BEYOND
FINANCIAL
FITNESS

BEYOND FINANCIAL FITNESS

HOW TO BUILD SECURITY AND PROSPERITY FOR THE FUTURE

NEW YORK TIMES BESTSELLING AUTHORS

CHRIS BRADY
ORRIN WOODWARD

OBSTACLÉS PRESS

Published by:

Obstaclés Press
200 Commonwealth Court
Cary, NC 27511

First Edition, July 2016
10 9 8 7 6 5 4 3 2 1

financialfitnessinfo.com

ISBN: 978-0-9976311-4-2

Library of Congress Control Number: 2016909919

Book design by Norm Williams, nwa-inc.com

Printed in the United States of America

In Memory of Denny Smith

CONTENTS

Preface

Many people, when confronted with the reality of their financial position, respond like an ostrich hunted by a lion and merely bury their heads in the sand. Others, in contrast, realize they must make some changes, but they get so mired in the defensive details that they lose the forest for the trees. Of course, both scenarios miss out on the true strength of the Financial Fitness Program (FFP). Many financial programs offer defensive strategies to help people get out of debt, but only the FFP describes the playing field rules *and* teaches how to win the financial game by combining defense and offense. After all, who wants to live on a financial diet the rest of their life while sacrificing dreams to be merely debt free? Is it possible to live debt free and still live the life of one's dreams? Yes, and teaching people how to do so is the very reason the Financial Fitness Program was created.

First, reader, you must understand that the financial system is rigged against you. It's not just a matter of the consumer lacking fiscal responsibility, although this certainly plays a part. The system itself is designed to profit the bankers and other financial intermediaries at the consumer's expense. For example, while banks are allowed to create mortgage loans out of thin air (through the wonders of the fractional reserve banking system), people are expected to pay back this money by surrendering a portion of the fruit of their productive labors for thirty years.

Of course, mortgage loans are just one of the devices the banking system uses to slither its tentacles around a person's pocketbook. Once student loans, car loans, car leases, credit cards, and consumer loans are added to the list, the amount of money going to service debt amounts to over 33 percent of a person's take-home income! Needless to say, paying 33 percent to the banking system for the privilege of accessing money created out of thin air seems like an unfair playing field. As we've written elsewhere, many people will spend the largest part of their lives working for something banks can create out of thin air in an instant.

Personal debt, however, is just one of the banking system's three-pronged approaches to bilking society: businesses and governments are also in debt up to their eyeballs. In fact, the St. Louis Federal Reserve Bank announced that the total US debt (the combination of government, business, mortgage, and consumer debt) had increased from $2.2 trillion in 1972 (the year President Nixon took the dollar off the international gold standard) to nearly $59.4 trillion in the first quarter of 2014. That's an unbelievable 27-fold increase! Interestingly, this gargantuan debt is split almost evenly among the three sectors with personal, business, and government debts totaling roughly $20 trillion each. Businesses cover their debt by raising prices, while governments cover theirs by raising taxes; but unfortunately, the consumer ends up footing the bill for both. It's no wonder citizens across the developed world are struggling.

Disastrously, even assuming a rate of just 5 percent, America's interest on its debt today amounts to over $3 trillion. That's 3,000,000,000,000 dollars! The money to pay this interest is siphoned off the top of the productive capacity of every American by the banking system that created it in the first place. In other words, before people are allowed to enjoy the fruits of their labor, they are forced to service everyone else's debts (personal, business, *and* government). The game is rigged. Ignorance of it only ensures financial failure in the long run.

The authors have named this fixed game the *Financial Matrix* (after the popular 1999 major motion picture). It's a system of control designed to enslave the unsuspecting while profiting those in charge. Unfortunately, the widespread lack of financial literacy allows this system to seduce people into debt enslavement. In reality, unlike earlier machinations that were based upon coercion (such as slavery or serfdom), the Financial Matrix is a system of control in which people freely choose their own bondage.

The world is in the midst of a debt deluge. Still, pessimism is not the answer. After all, although no one can control what governments or businesses do, everyone *can* learn to stop being seduced into debt slavery. This alone would return 33 percent of most people's income to their control. This is where the importance of learning how to play defense comes into play. Defense, simply stated, is spending less than one makes. The difference between what one makes and what one spends can then be applied to the remaining debt until it is eliminated. It's amazing how simple it all sounds but also how difficult it is to stop being seduced into indentured service for the latest "shiny object."

Interestingly, however, most financial literacy programs cover little, if anything, of the playing field and instead focus mainly on the defensive steps. While defense is good, no one can win a sports championship without also having offense. The same is true in personal finance. Strangely, most programs are silent on crucial aspects of the financial game. Hence, a typical financial education directs your focus to your current reality. Naturally, this keeps your head down in the details and dirt of your present financial mess.

The problem with a solely defensive financial mind-set is that it gets you thinking so logically about scrimping today that you forget to dream about a better tomorrow. In contrast, a proper financial plan should lead you to look down into the details in order to develop today's belt-tightening plan—but then compel you to *look up* so you can *get up*. After all, the goal is not for you to surrender your dreams in order to live debt free. Rather, the goal is for you to live below your means so you can begin investing, as Warren Buffett said, in your number one resource, namely, your personal development.

Indeed, developing personal and professional skills is essential for offense. Why this is not customarily emphasized in a person's financial plan is inexplicable, especially when one considers that there are only two methods to increase the amount remaining between what one makes and one spends: either make more or spend less. As a result, both the *make more* (offense) and the *spend less* (defense) are vital. To make more money, however, a person must dream for a better future and then follow it up by investing in more skills. If one wants to change what one earns, one must correspondingly change what one can contribute. Interestingly, the skills most highly prized are not the "hard" technical skills but rather the "soft" people skills. Many gain the technical skills but lack the people skills to convey their ideas and work as part of a healthy team. Above all else, improving people skills is the fastest way to increase one's income. For instance, Dale Carnegie once wrote, "15 percent of one's financial success is due to one's technical knowledge and about 85 percent is due to skill in human engineering—to personality and the ability to lead people." Warren Buffett himself displays his Dale Carnegie course completion certificate proudly on his office wall (rather than his undergraduate and master's degrees).

A person may believe that Carnegie's words, written back in 1936, are no longer valid in today's highly technical age. But if anything, people skills are needed today more than ever. For instance, even the technology giant Google realized that technical skills alone did not make for a good manager. According to Google Vice President Laszlo Bock, "In the Google context, we'd always believed that to be a manager, particularly on the engineering side, you needed to be as deep or deeper a technical expert than the people who work for you. It turns out that that's absolutely the least important thing. It's important, but pales in comparison. Much more important is just making that connection and being accessible."

This is the where the Financial Fitness Program shines above all others. For not only does it teach the mostly common sense principles of defense, but it also encourages the attainment of offensive skills, while making the participant aware of the harsh reality of the rules of the "playing field." No other program seeks to educate across all three of these critical areas.

Know this: the real secret to going *beyond* financial fitness is to develop a burning desire. In contrast to getting buried in defensive details for the next twenty years, true financial offense teaches a person how to dream and achieve. Perhaps never before has Napoleon Hill's advice from his classic *Think and Grow Rich* been more indispensable: "There is one quality which one must possess to win, and that is definiteness of purpose, the knowledge of what one wants, and a burning desire to possess it." Indeed, a burning desire turns fantasies into dreams and dreams into achievable goals.

Unfortunately, most people live their lives as wandering generalities rather than as specific intentionalities. After all, success can be boiled down to three questions: (1) What do you want? (2) What does it cost? (3) Will you pay it? The burning desire is what helps a person answer these three critical questions to help him or her live a life of purpose in an age of purposelessness. A burning desire turns a someday fantasy into a dream with a deadline, through the power of goal setting today. Success, as they said of Rome, isn't built in a day, but it *is* built day by day.

The financial education presented in these pages will give you the equipment you need to start building your proverbial Rome, one productive day at a time. You *can* live the life you've always wanted by going *beyond* financial fitness.

INTRODUCTION

"It is easy in the world to live after the world's opinion; it is easy in solitude to live after our own; but the great man is he who in the midst of the crowd keeps with perfect sweetness the independence of solitude."
—RALPH WALDO EMERSON

Early in the movie *99 Homes* there is a chilling eviction scene in which a single father and his mother are being ousted from their family home. The stress builds as the scene plays out. The neighbors wander out into their yards to see what all the commotion is about. Blue-collar laborers lean against trucks waiting to enter the home and cart the families' belongings to the curb. Two policemen assist in the proceedings. As it becomes clearer and clearer to the young man and his middle-aged mother that they are powerless against the law, their anger intensifies. A confused discussion turns into a shouting match, with the law enforcement officials becoming increasingly firm in their demands. Then, in the middle of it all, the man's adolescent son gets off the school bus and wanders sheepishly into the chaos as his friends look on. Given mere minutes to gather any personal effects, the man and his mother are told they must step to the other side of the sidewalk, as they are now trespassing on what they had mere moments before considered their own property. After agonizing minutes, the scene finally ends with the trio driving off in an awkwardly loaded pickup truck searching for a cheap motel to stay in for the night.

Anyone who has ever experienced financial stress can relate to the tension in that scene. There is nothing quite like the oppressive power of money problems to weigh us down and produce the worst kind of torment in our lives. Debt, credit problems, collections agencies, foreclosures, penalties and fees, and, yes, evictions are not just the stuff of dramatic films. They happen to real people in real life every day.

Financial Fitness

For the purpose of helping those trapped in such a struggle, we several years ago produced the *Financial Fitness* book and accompanying suite of products. It was designed to prevent people from ever having to experience the very kind of event so realistically depicted in that movie. Since the release of those materials, we've heard from hundreds and hundreds of satisfied customers who have significantly or entirely eliminated the debt stress in their lives.

"Because of the Financial Fitness Program, we own ALL of our vehicles free and clear, all 12 of our credit cards are paid off and gone and all of our personal loans are gone—including a Chevy truck loan we had to take out when our 1993 vehicle died. To date, we have paid off over $50,000 of debt. It's scary how the 'agents' of the Financial Matrix work; I'm still amazed at how much the banks were willing to 'give' us to finance our life."—Wendy Stout

"After 2 years of learning from and implementing the Financial Fitness Program, we were able to pay off both of our cars, all of our student loans, all of our credit cards and all of our medical bills and at the same time put money into an emergency fund and savings account. In total, we have paid off over $40,000 in debt and now have a savings account balance with a comma!"—Keith and Lynn Burns

"The biggest turning point for me in learning from the Financial Fitness Program was realizing that I didn't have to stay in debt; there was a way out! All I had to do was be a student, learn and apply the principles by analyzing my bad habits and breaking those habits and developing new and better ones."—Jean Finney

"If we hadn't been introduced to the Financial Fitness Program, I don't know where we'd be today. Not only has it been the best, but it has been the only program that has worked for us."—Robby Palmer

"It has been documented that the average American has less than $500 in a savings account. That was us before Financial Fitness. By practicing the basic principle of paying ourselves first, we were able to grow an actual savings account 5000% that just a few short years ago would have been the equivalent to winning the lottery for us. It's just crazy what a little financial literacy can do for you."—Mike Burns[1]

The success of the Financial Fitness material in the hands of people who were suffering from overbearing money problems has been wonderful to see. As a matter of fact, while watching *99 Homes*, we couldn't have been more proud of the stand we have taken against needless consumer debt and the strategy of financial education to set people free from what we call the Financial Matrix.

---

1   The people quoted in this book are not actors nor have they been paid to participate. They are real people that have used the products and services and have signed testimonial verifications attesting to the validity of their statements.

As related in the Preface, the Financial Matrix is a reference to another movie, *The Matrix*, which depicted the world as an elaborate charade designed to keep people trapped in their belief that it was real. The whole world was rigged in order to exploit people who didn't even realize they were being exploited. Financially speaking, there is a strong argument to be made that much the same is happening in our world as regards (especially) the middle class: the people who work hard at jobs or small businesses for a living, get mortgages so they can afford homes, struggle to pay to educate their children, and do their best just to survive.

At some point during their years of strife, many come to feel that the deck is stacked against them. How could working so hard for so long accomplish so little, when others seem to easily rise above the challenges and find real wealth? As the gap between the wealthy and the rest gets wider and wider, more and more people realize that some type of Financial Matrix is indeed real and in play. The result of such angst is movements such as the Wall Street protests, populist momentum in politics, or general apathy and the desire to just give up and go into debt even further.

But there is a better answer.

Learning about money and becoming its master instead of its slave is part one of that answer. Avoiding real-life evictions and financial stress is what we call the *defense* side of learning about money. It involves understanding the power of debt against our efforts in life, how creditors consider us to be their assets, and how the compounding power of debt

> **Those who don't understand the power of compound interest are destined to pay it.**

interest is a tiger that intensifies in his ferocity as time goes on. As one financier put it, "Those who don't understand the power of compound interest are destined to pay it." The defense section of our Financial Fitness training concentrates on helping people get out of debt and stay out of debt, developing productive habits that, over time, can help them beat the Financial Matrix. This is what those satisfied customers and readers we quoted above have done, and their relief is palpable. There is nothing like getting out of debt and owing no one anywhere any money whatsoever. In fact, if you've never experienced that feeling of independence, we highly recommend that you get your hands on the *Financial Fitness* book and/or program, and apply its principles to your life.

But defense is only one part of three in the mastery of money. The other two parts, uniquely taught in the Financial Fitness program, are *offense* and the *playing field*. Offense is the idea that in order to truly get ahead financially in life, we need to not only learn how to keep more of what we make (defense), but also learn how to make more as well (offense). The trite statement is that in order to get wealthy one must spend less than one makes *and* make more than one spends. Defense is the first part, and offense is the second.

Finally, the playing field refers to the forces at work in the Financial Matrix and how they affect every single aspect of our financial lives. This includes considerations like inflation, interest rates, market volatility, tax laws, investment strategies, and a whole gamut of factors that play into our overall ability to get ahead financially. As you grow in your financial standing, these forces, and knowing how to account for them, will become more and more important.

The YOU, Inc. Investment Hierarchy

While the Financial Fitness program is a complete package that focuses on all three parts of personal finance (defense, offense, and the playing field), it is not the complete story. In chapter 15 of the original *Financial Fitness* book, we introduce something we called the *YOU, Inc. Investment Hierarchy*. This is simply a graphical representation of the priorities of where to focus your money, depending upon your particular progress on your journey to financial fitness. The idea is that the bottom of the hierarchy is the most important (and therefore drawn the largest) and should get the lion's share of your focus as you start out (and continually as you go further up the hierarchy, never leaving any of the levels behind). However, in the original book and program, we were space-constrained and prevented from doing much more than providing a cursory look into the hierarchy and how it applies to someone's offensive strategy. Since then, we have repeatedly been asked by customers and readers who have successfully applied the concepts, and thereby ascended the hierarchy, to provide further detail and education on the higher levels of the structure. That, in short, is the purpose of this book.

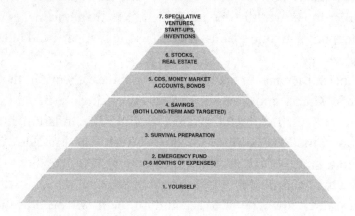

The original work provides the foundational education regarding how to get out of debt and stay out of debt, develop good habits of money management, perhaps even start additional streams of income through personal business ownership, and then begin flowing the results into the YOU, Inc. Hierarchy. If you haven't mastered these steps, we suggest you get your hands on a copy of the *Financial Fitness* book and/or program and apply them to your life immediately. However, even if you haven't, you will still gain a lot from the material in this publication, as it will begin with a review of some of the key ingredients of the Financial Fitness training before building up from there. However, the primary focus of this material is to extend the concepts of the original work and effectively take the information *beyond* Financial Fitness and upward toward real prosperity and security. In short, this book covers the many details involved in scaling the upper heights of the YOU, Inc. Hierarchy. It will take you from merely becoming financially fit, to "bulking up" and going beyond fitness to something else entirely.

At the risk of using too many metaphors and movies to describe these concepts, we will go with one more. If Financial Fitness is exactly what it sounds like—eliminating the flab of debt and getting lean and mean with your money—then going *beyond* Financial Fitness is a lot like what we do when we begin to build physical muscle. It's one thing to lose weight and get fit; it's another to start intentionally building muscle and making yourself stronger and faster. That's the analogy here. The *Financial Fitness* book and program were designed to help you lose the debt flab and get to your target weight of zero debt. *Beyond Financial Fitness* will teach you to build muscle beyond anything you've ever built before. We will take you into a whole gymnasium of equipment designed for just that purpose.

Just like building real physical muscles, this work takes time and attention and dedication. But as with the physical example, when you can look in the mirror and admire the progress you've made with visible proof of your efforts, much the same can happen with your finances. Your efforts to build on your new, slender, fit financial situation will show up in your lifestyle. Just like those new biceps or quads that can't be hidden when you take your stroll at the beach, financial prosperity is pretty hard to hide as well. And having it can be almost as much fun as showcasing that taut beach body!

The Three Considerations of the Intelligent Investor

Nearly everyone has heard of Warren Buffett (mentioned above), one of the world's richest individuals and possibly the most famous investor of all time. Buffett's Midwestern persona and public congeniality endear him to people in all walks of life, and his popularity has brought attention to an investment strategy known as value investing. What many people may not know is that Buffett did not invent himself out of whole cloth; he actually attributes much of his success to a mentor named Benjamin Graham. Graham is widely regarded as the father of value investing. Much later in the book, we will get into what value investing is, as well as other types of investing, but suffice it to say that Benjamin Graham wrote the book on investing—literally! In what Warren Buffett calls "by far the best book on investing ever written," Graham's *The Intelligent Investor* (along with commentary by another money expert, Jason Zweig) spells out the three main tools people need in order to properly build beyond financial fitness:

1. A *Comprehensive Financial Plan* that outlines how you will earn, save, spend, borrow, and invest your money.
2. An *Investment Policy* that spells out your fundamental approach to investing.
3. An *Asset Allocation Plan* that details how much money you will keep in different investment categories.

If it's good enough for Graham, Zweig, and Buffett, it's good enough for us! This book will be arranged around those same three categories. By the time you finish studying this material, you'll know how to readily put all three in place. You won't just be fit; you'll be learning how to be financially buff! And just as with the physical comparison, how far you go and how much financial muscle you build will be up to you. This book will give you the keys to the gym.

PART I

COMPREHENSIVE FINANCIAL PLAN

HOW YOU WILL EARN, SAVE, SPEND, BORROW, AND INVEST YOUR MONEY

ONE

Having the Right Idea about Money

"Rich men use most of their money to get richer.
Poor men use most of their money to look richer"
—Mokokoma Mokhonoana

In our years of dealing with people and their finances, we have discovered one overriding observation: many people have no idea what money is really *for*. Their understanding of money and its purpose is 100 percent, entirely, totally, and emphatically wrong. They think money is something to be used to buy what they want. For them, the relationship goes like this: get some money, spend it to buy stuff. When they want more stuff, they get more money and spend it on that stuff. Make money, buy stuff. Make more money, buy more stuff. And on it goes. They see people in nice cars and big houses and assume those people must have more money than someone in a used car and a smaller house. They quickly learn about mortgages and credit cards and student loans, and they ante up, putting themselves in debt (like everyone else) and assuming that it is all normal. After all, if "everybody is doing it," it must be right. It must be "the way things are done."

But this is all wrong. It is what we call a *middle class mind-set* about money. It results in becoming a slave to money instead of the other way around. A middle class mind-set keeps someone working at a job they don't necessarily love to pay bills they can't handle because they bought things they couldn't afford with money they didn't yet have. It means having the wrong view of money: a view that enslaves one to credit and debt and takes its toll as the years go by, as there just doesn't seem to be enough money to make ends meet.

Now don't get us wrong. There are quite often legitimate occurrences in our financial lives that throw us off kilter. We get hit with medical emergencies, job losses, or the need to take care of loved ones, and sometimes the magnitude of these challenges can drain our coffers and hurt our finances. We understand these events and know they can put people in real financial peril. But that is not what we're talking about here. We're referring to people who are under money pressure constantly, who can't seem to make ends meet year after year, who are in debt for consumer items, and who can't seem to get their proverbial heads above water. We're referring to millions and millions of people who live this way every day, systematically, by default. And the tragic thing about it is that they don't have to live this way. It doesn't have to be like this.

There is another group of people who are *time* poor. They make plenty of money from high paying jobs, but they too seem to be lacking something. It isn't necessarily *items* they lack; rather, it's *time* (and maybe stress-free moments). These are the people who, in the eyes of others, at least, have "made it." They have the high-status position, or they work in a sexy profession, but it takes a big toll on them to do what they do. It is stressful to be them and to produce what they produce. Sure, they've got some debt, but they can afford the payments, and after all the hassle they go through to earn their money, they can easily justify to themselves a few nice splurges. They're certainly not broke. But in honest moments, these high fliers often tell us they feel trapped. They feel as if they are missing something. They feel "broke," if just at a higher level. They make plenty of money, but it seems to disappear all too quickly. They are either time broke, or money broke at a high level, or both.

Finally, for both groups, there is a total lack of preparedness for old age and/or retirement. The statistics, which we'll spare you, are shocking. Having too little saved for one's "golden years" is almost an international cliché. It's like being told we don't eat enough vegetables or that we should drink more water. "Yeah, yeah," our minds seem to say. "We've heard it all before. I've got enough to worry about today; I'll get to that some other day." But this is a real problem with scary consequences for millions of people.

We don't mean to offend anybody. We're speaking in generalities only and don't wish to label anyone. But a lack of financial literacy characterizes most of the people we've worked with for going on twenty-five years. The common denominator is the position money has in people's lives: in essence, a position of *control*. Actually, money shouldn't have control over *them*; they should instead have control over *money*. And instead of working *for* money, they ought to have money working *for them*. In order to achieve this, one must get the right understanding of money in the first place.

The Crank

Let's see if a simple diagram will help illustrate what we are trying to say. Below is a hand crank pump. It's pretty simple, really: you turn the crank and it pumps water. Stop cranking and eventually the water stops flowing. Want more water? Turn the crank some more. This is how most people see money. They turn a crank to get some money flowing. Then they can take that money and spend it on stuff they want. To get more money, they just turn the crank some more, and then more money comes out that they can also spend. That's it—day after day, month after month, year after year.

Buy Stuff

Of course, there are variations on this theme. Some get more efficient pumps by going to college and thereby getting a higher paying crank. Then, once they have that mighty college degree, they can turn the crank and get *more* money out each time. In fact, the game seems to be to get the best education possible, so that one can get the best job possible and in so doing maximize the amount of money flowing out of the pump.

This is exactly how the authors looked at the world when we came out of college with a collection of engineering degrees and well-paying professional jobs. We were quite sure we had "made it" and would now spend a life of bliss earning big bucks from the turning of our cranks. In fact, our wives were also professionals who had their own money pumps, so we were dead certain life would be one big lucrative money stream from there on out— dead certain, but dead wrong.

The problem was that no matter how much money-flow we pumped as a result of our cranking, it all got spent. And then some beyond that. Some of it went to student loans, some to mortgage payments, some to car payments, and in one embarrassing instance, payments on a "sticky wood" pressboard desk. The monthly interest on all these loan payments was enormous and ate heartily into our take-home pay.

Also, with high-paying jobs and nice fat W2s (a document the United States government requires employers to issue showing how much each employee earned that year in wages), our tax picture wasn't all that great either. Without any meaningful deductions, we paid huge sums of money to the federal government, into Social Security, to our state government, and to our local governments. After paying these taxes and the loans and the interest on the loans, it's little wonder we weren't getting ahead. Eventually, a kind of futility began to set in, and we *almost* surrendered to the conclusion that we would always be in debt, and if we wanted to have anything nice we'd just have to finance it like everyone else. *Almost.*

ESBI

Sometime in our late twenties we went into business together. In so doing, we tried to find mentors and information to teach us how to succeed. It wasn't easy going. We tried very hard for a long time. But the situation gradually began to work out. Our understanding about money and investing and building something for the long term grew. We shed many of our incorrect views about money and began to prosper. Somewhere along the way we were introduced to an author and educator who helped clarify the picture for us. His name was Robert Kiyosaki, and our breakthrough came from something he called the *Cashflow Quadrant* (taken from the book of the same name).

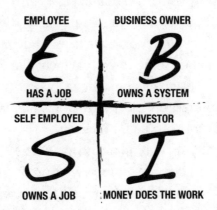

In this ingeniously simple little diagram, Kiyosaki teaches some profound truths. According to Kiyosaki, the left side of the diagram represents about 90 percent of the people and 10 percent of the wealth. The right side is just the opposite, 10 percent of the people and about 90 percent of the wealth.

The four letters, one in each quadrant, represent four different ways of making money.

The *E* stands for *employee*. This is someone who trades his or her time and skills for a wage. The goal is to gain as much pay as possible for the time put into the job. This person has a job and is basically paid directly for the time spent there.

The *S* stands for *self-employed* or *small business owner*. This represents the individual who had the guts to step out and basically take ownership of a job itself. Instead of a boss paying for tasks, this person has customers paying for those tasks. This person is paid per service performed and could be said to "own a job."

The *B* stands for *big business* or *B-type business*. This represents an entity that makes money whether the owners are there or not. It is run by a system and not directly by a person. If an E person has a job, and an S person owns a job, then a person who makes his or her living in the B quadrant owns a *system* that does the work.

Finally, the *I* represents *investing*. This is the situation in which money earns more money for its owner. Those in the I quadrant have put *money* to work for them.

This diagram was a major breakthrough for us. It demonstrated that there were drastically different approaches to the getting of money, and that there were advantages and disadvantages to each. For instance, an employee would not necessarily be stressed out by all the responsibilities of ownership of the income source, but the income would be limited by someone else's decisions. An S business owner would have more input into his or her income level, but more stress because he or she would own the enterprise. However, it was clear that both the E and the S individual would be limited by their time.

By contrast, the B type business owner would not have to trade his or her time for dollars, as in the case of both the E and the S, but it was obvious that setting up such a situation would not be easy or quickly done. And finally, the investor would need sufficient funds and expertise to make returns on that money possible.

It all became clear to us, a path we could travel from where we were to where we wanted to go. We could begin as employees, gradually working our way part-time to small business ownership, and then setting up systems to run our business automatically even when we weren't there, turning it into a B-type business. Ultimately, excess profits could be channeled into the I quadrant, which would make even more money for us.

That was our particular path *beyond* financial fitness. But there are many combinations of these. And just to be clear, there is no right and wrong quadrant. People are all different, with different skills, desires, and life callings. Some will do what we did; others will happily stay in the E quadrant. Some will gravitate from the E to the S. Others will work from the E while investing funds in the I. It all works. It just has to suit your particular situation and desires.

Beyond the details of the various quadrants and the different ways of making money, the Cashflow Quadrant actually shows us one more very important thing. It shows us what the wealthy do.

To explain, let's go back to our crank pump diagram. Only this time, let's make one slight modification. Instead of the flow from the pump being used *primarily* to buy the stuff we want, let's direct a portion of that flow toward the building and accumulation of assets. What is an asset? *An asset is anything that brings you more money.* It may grow in time or flow money right away, but overall, an asset is something that takes your dollars (or euros or pesos or yen) and multiplies them.

Accumulate Assets

Building and Accumulating Assets

Now we're going to just come out and say it: money is not for buying what you want. Only a *part* of it is for that. Money is for much *more* than that. Money is for buying freedom and security, too. Money is for serving one's life purpose. Money is for giving and blessing others. Money is for leaving a legacy and for the giving of gifts. Money is for protection and safety, travel and experience, memories and more.

Money is vastly more than just a medium of exchange for buying stuff that you want. It is ideally a little worker that you employ to go out and bring back more little workers just like it. The problem is, if one thinks that money is only for the buying of stuff, then it won't be treated properly, will not be cared for diligently, and will not be funneled into growth opportunities from which it can bring back more money.

From studying the Cashflow Quadrant, we see that the right side is where most of the wealth is, which means we would be wise to put effort toward building up either the B or the I quadrant (or both) continually over time. Just as the authors moved through the whole diagram, from one quadrant to another and then another, it can be profitable for anyone to take the fruits of his or her labor and apply them to more than one of the situations represented by the Cashflow Quadrant.

For instance, an employee working in the E quadrant can funnel off some of her earnings and place them in sound investments in the I quadrant, feeding something that will grow nicely over time. The same can be done for an S business owner or a B-type business owner. In fact, we would recommend that no matter which of the other three quadrants in which you make your money, some of that money should always (or at least eventually) be flowing into the I quadrant. Or perhaps you are working a job as an employee and investing your extra money to build an S business that is your heart's desire. Or maybe you're trying to take the money from your S business and use it to develop systems that will turn that business into a B-type business. All of these moves are essentially the use of your money toward the building of assets, playing the money game the way the wealthy do, and putting effort into building up resources on the right side of the quadrant. This is the fundamental path that will take you from mere financial fitness to something beyond.

> **Your goal should be to get by on only a portion of the money you earn so that the rest can be put into efforts to multiply itself.**

Your goal should be to get by on only a portion of the money you earn so that the rest can be put into efforts to multiply itself. This is the exact opposite of what most people do with their money. As stated above, people's completely wrong understanding of what money is for leads them to waste it by buying stuff to satisfy their need for short-term gratification. Not only do they *not* funnel large portions of what they earn over to the right side of the Cashflow Quadrant, but worse, they actually spend beyond their means and go into debt. Then, through the interest payments owed on this debt, they effectively become someone else's asset and their own liability. Instead of building assets, they become someone else's asset. As one of our grandfathers used to say, "It's not enough that we cut off our own arm, we are also beating ourselves over the head with the bloody end of it!"

> **Here is a secret of the wealthy: *they use their money to acquire assets.***

Here is a secret of the wealthy: *they use their money to acquire assets.* This bears restating: *the chief purpose of your money is to build and acquire assets.* These assets then grow and accumulate over time. It is the cash flow from the ownership of these assets that can give you the life you've always wanted.

When we talk about putting together a Comprehensive Financial Plan, as Benjamin Graham recommends, step one in that process is realizing the proper use of money and determining that you will commit to flowing some of it (and hopefully as much as you possibly can), on a regular basis, toward the accumulation of assets. How best to do that is what we'll be teaching you throughout the rest of the book.

TWO

Directing the
Cash Flow

*"Those who do not understand the power of
compound interest are doomed to pay it."*
—ANONYMOUS

*T*he *Richest Man in Babylon*, one of the best-selling financial
books of all time, teaches the very simple but important concept of "paying oneself first." The idea is that a portion of all the
money you earn is yours to keep. Tactically, this is accomplished
by placing a portion of all of your income, each and every time
you receive it, immediately into a savings account (or other appropriate asset-building destination; we'll discuss the many options later).

The best way to do this is to set it up to happen automatically,
using any of today's options of direct deposit, so that every time
you get paid, a portion of that money goes straight into your asset column. As this happens month in and month out, over time,
the accumulation can be quite pleasing. Additionally, thanks to
the power of compound interest, if you consistently place such
funds into an account where interest is allowed to do its magic,
the growth over your lifetime will be downright stunning.

This simple little step has many benefits. The first is that you
are keeping money away from your most dangerous financial

adversary—you! Yes, it's true, many people are their own worst enemy when it comes to their personal finances. They just can't help spending every dime they make. But if you set up a direct deposit of a portion of your income each and every time you receive it and place that money where you can't easily get your hands on it, you will be bypassing the temptation to squander those funds and thereby protecting them from yourself.

Another big benefit is the habit this instills. Being able to do something so productive on a consistent basis is a sure sign of financial maturity, and it will instill confidence that you can indeed build something significant over time. Also, by paying yourself first this way, you begin to reorient your vision toward the long term. Instead of thinking only of what money can buy you today, you begin to realize how much good it can do once it has grown bigger for tomorrow. Ultimately, though, the advantage to paying yourself first is that this becomes a source of funds from which you can start building up assets, as we introduced in the previous chapter.

This procedure sounds simple, but that doesn't mean it's easy. Many find it difficult to believe that they can get by without a portion of their income each month. And at first, they may feel a pinch as they make the necessary sacrifice to live on a little less. But we promise, in a surprisingly short time, the money won't even be missed, and your life will go on just fine without it.

Others object to this idea because it isn't flashy enough for them. It doesn't involve anything dramatic or come with any measure of status. It just seems too simple to be that powerful, they think.

Let us remind you of the popular but still compelling example of the penny that doubles every day. It is the best illustration of the power of small things to multiply over time that we have ever encountered. In the math one can certainly see why Einstein quipped that the power of compound interest should be considered to be the Eighth Wonder of the World.

To demonstrate how "compounding" works, consider the following famous scenario in which a penny is doubled every day for thirty days:

Day 1: 1 penny
Day 2: 2 pennies
Day 3: 4 pennies
Day 4: 8 pennies
Day 5: 16 pennies
Day 6: 32 pennies
Day 7: 64 pennies
Day 8: $1.28
Day 9: $2.56
Day 10: $5.12
Day 11: $10.24
Day 12: $20.48
Day 13: $40.96
Day 14: $81.92
Day 15: $163.84
Day 16: $327.68
Day 17: $655.36
Day 18: $1,310.72
Day 19: $2,621.44
Day 20: $5,242.88
Day 21: $10,485.76
Day 22: $20,971.52
Day 23: $41,943.04
Day 24: $83,886.08
Day 25: $167,772.16
Day 26: $335,544.32
Day 27: $671,088.64
Day 28: $1,342,177.28
Day 29: $2,684,354.56
Day 30: $5,368,709.12

Now, add up the entire amount for each of the thirty days and it comes to $10,737,089.91! That's the power of compounding.

It is by such little steps that money consistently contributed directly from your earnings into some interest-bearing account can multiply and grow. It is worth your time, worth a little sac-rifice, and worth not overlooking as too simple. The principle of "paying yourself first" works, and it is one of the foundational steps toward accumulating assets and building real wealth.

Directing the Flows

To understand how to best apply the principle of paying your-self first, let's return to our hand crank pump diagram from the previous chapter.

You'll remember that turning the crank on this pump repre-sents what you do to earn your money with your job and/or busi-ness. The concept of paying yourself first involves automatically and consistently channeling some of the cash flow from your money pump into asset accumulation.

In our original *Financial Fitness* book, we recommended that to begin with, this money go toward the establishment of what we called an *emergency fund*. This is a separate bank account that you open for the sole purpose of just what it sounds like: preparation for an emergency. This might be a critical medical situation, a broken furnace, loss of employment, or other such unforeseen but harsh financial need. Almost any financial adviser you consult will tell you to take this very important step. Many experts say that the most common reason people who have gotten out of debt get back *into* debt is because of having to use credit cards in an emergency.

Based upon your income level and financial stability, your exact recommendation may differ, but we generally encourage people to funnel money into this account until it contains at least three to six months of their current monthly expenses. This means that you could lose your primary source of income and be okay for that period of time. Depending upon your particular income situation or tolerance for risk, you may want to build this account even larger. But beginning with three to six months is a good start.

Next, once the emergency fund has been established, the money that you are automatically paying yourself first should then be channeled into regular savings. Part of this is for the long term (meaning you really never touch it; more on this later); and part of it can be for what we call *targeted savings*. Targeted savings is money you set aside in order to be able to afford a future purchase. It may be a health care savings account, a college savings account, or just money you are trying to stack up so you can buy a new car when the time is right. We will talk in more detail later about these and other options, but just know at this point that once you've established your emergency fund, you keep going with the concept of paying your-

> In essence, you never stop paying yourself first; you just change where it goes as time passes.

self first and funnel it into other things. In essence, you never stop paying yourself first; you just change where it goes as time passes.

The YOU, Inc. Investment Hierarchy

In the Introduction we mentioned the concept of the YOU, Inc. Investment Hierarchy. This diagram is a simple representation of the priorities of your money flow as you channel it from your money pump into the accumulation of assets. It's called YOU, Inc. for a reason. This is because it is most helpful for accumulating assets for the long term and achieving your lifetime financial goals if you think of yourself as the CEO of your own corporation. Think about what a CEO does: she manages the resources of a company for maximum customer satisfaction and stakeholder return. When considering how you can manage your money to its fullest potential, mimicking this corporate attitude is exactly what is most productive. The monies coming in are the resources. The customers are the people you and your family come into contact with in life and those affected by the services and contribution to society you provide. The stakeholders are you and your loved ones (possibly for generations to come). A life lived *beyond* mere financial fitness involves the mature and responsible allocation of your money flow into the uses that will best serve the overall needs and higher purpose for your life. In short, you will be acting as the CEO for your own financial life.

> A life lived *beyond* mere financial fitness involves the mature and responsible allocation of your money flow into the uses that will best serve the overall needs and higher purpose for your life.

With that understanding, let's consider the bottom four levels of the YOU, Inc. Hierarchy.

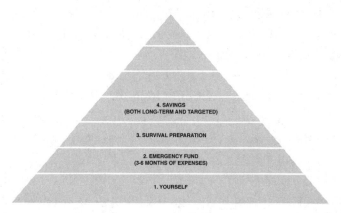

Since we covered this extensively in the *Financial Fitness* book, we won't go into it much here. But suffice it to say that the lowest level of the YOU, Inc. Hierarchy is the first and the largest for a reason. Investing in yourself is and always will be the best investment you can ever make. Perhaps that means obtaining an education to make you more marketable or investing in personal development and acquiring the "soft skills" that are crucial for success in working with others. It may mean investing in the tools and inventory of a business you are building. The details will be different for every individual case, but the principle is universal: investing in yourself first and always is the best investment you can ever make. This is because you are totally in control of the outcome, and anything that builds you builds your ability to fulfill your life's purpose, which is one of the biggest reasons to invest and grow assets to begin with! Therefore, never hesitate to channel some of your money into this category of investing. It will always pay the biggest dividends in life.

Moving up the hierarchy, we can see that next comes the emergency fund we've already discussed. Once this is funded for the three to six months of your expenses, your next move, Level 3, is to take care of a little survival preparation. We offer this step with a bit of a wince, as we have seen people get way too apocalyptic here. We don't mean building a bomb shelter and bunker full of bullets and booze (although that may get you featured on one of those reality TV shows) but more realistically just stocking away some useful things in preparation for a true emergency. It never hurts to be prepared.

The fourth level of the YOU, Inc. Hierarchy is savings. As we already stated, this includes both long-term and targeted funds. These should be held separately and probably in different types of accounts. We will get into much more detail on the types of accounts in chapter 6.

Let's revisit the money pump once again, this time showing how the cash flow coming from the pump is channeled into the YOU, Inc. Hierarchy. Before, we were simply saying that your money flow should be directed into the accumulation of assets, but as you can see, the YOU, Inc. Hierarchy is actually our roadmap for how to direct those funds. One should work from the bottom up, the bottom being first and widest because it is the most important. One you've invested all you can in yourself and your business and/or profession (something you should never stop doing all the years of your life), the rest of the money can flow upward into the higher levels of the hierarchy, first filling the emergency fund, then the survival preparation, and then into both types of savings.

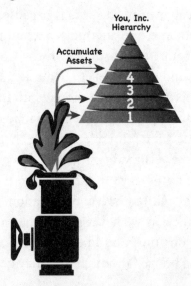

Giving

There is another flow which cannot be ignored that we must add to the diagram: the flow of your money into giving. We also covered this in depth in the *Financial Fitness* book, but it is worth revisiting here. Giving is one of life's biggest blessings, and also one of its deepest obligations. When we are blessed with money, even

> When we are blessed with money, even the tiniest amount, we are duty-bound to become a blessing *with* a portion of that money.

the tiniest amount, we are duty-bound to become a blessing *with* a portion of that money. When we are blessed, we should become a blessing. Besides, giving is one of the healthiest things anyone can do for herself. In addition to the countless people and causes that can be served by the giving of money, consider the many studies that suggest how healthy it is for the giver herself.

Further, the Bible is very clear that giving should be a pervasive spirit in how we live. Many religions agree, and interpretations range from giving a tithe (10 percent) of "first fruits" to spiritual giving which entails giving even more as one feels led to do so. In short, giving is commanded in many religions and encouraged almost everywhere in society, and for good reason: *it's just the right thing to do*. Consider at least a 10 percent regular giving from your money pump, and just as with "paying yourself first," this should be set up to happen automatically every time and immediately when you receive income.

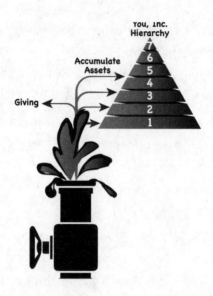

The Foundation under the Hierarchy

We've already covered a little bit about consumer debt. But let's take a look at just why it's so detrimental to one's financial life.

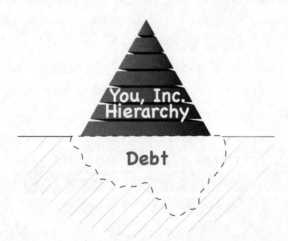

Consider the YOU, Inc. Investment Hierarchy as representing the large edifice of your future financial life. The goal is to build this structure to be massive, big enough to support all your life's purposes and dreams and goals. But as with any building, it must

46

rest on a firm foundation. When someone has consumer debt, he has a crater underneath any financial structure he attempts to build. In short, without getting out of debt, he is severely limiting his ability to build up assets over time. Even if some assets are acquired, they will be standing on a shaky foundation that could cause the whole thing to crumble. It happens time and time again.

When we strongly encourage people to get rid of their consumer debt (and to reject this way of living), we are trying to help them establish a firm foundation upon which their future wealth can grow. It is hard to build assets when you yourself are someone else's asset. If you are paying interest on loans, someone else has categorized the receiving of that interest on their books as an asset.

> **It is hard to build assets when you yourself are someone else's asset.**

Banks even bundle such debt and sell it as marketable securities. The debt of consumers thereby becomes the cash flow that contributes to a whole world of speculation and money games, all because someone had to buy something with money they didn't have, and they were willing to surrender future money (and interest payments on top of that) in order to get the item in the moment. Author and financial expert Liz Davidson wrote, "The safest and most profitable investment is one that no advisor can make for you. Only you can make this investment—which is to pay off your bad debt before you do anything else. In short, before you can start to accumulate wealth, you need to first take care of unwanted debt."

Depending upon the interest rates on some of your personal debt, getting rid of it might just represent the highest "returns" you will ever get in your investing life! Think about it: You are entirely in charge of eliminating negative interest working against you in your life. Nobody can prevent you from paying it off, and

47

nobody can make you ever get into such debt again. By taking control of this part of your finances and digging yourself out once and for all, you've established a firm foundation upon which to begin building your YOU, Inc. Hierarchy.

Nice Stuff and Junky Stuff

We have noticed a curious thing over the years. People who have large consumer debt generally do not have very much to show for it, while people who are debt free seem to have all the nice stuff. How can this be? Shouldn't those who buy nice stuff up front using credit have a bunch of cool things to show for it, while those miserly money-savers and practitioners of delayed gratification have nothing but worn-out clothing and junky cars? Right?

Not necessarily. The graph below shows why.

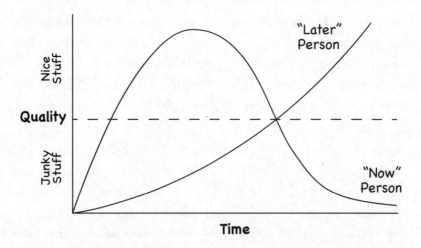

This graph represents two very different types of people. The "Now" person buys whatever he wants on credit. If he can afford the payment, he thinks he can afford the purchase. As a result, he goes out and buys "Nice Stuff" whenever he can. There is no delayed gratification here, as he wants what he wants when he wants it. And with the ease of obtaining credit today, he is able to get away with this—for a while.

The "Later" person does just the opposite. She waits until she can afford something before buying it, saving up the money and paying cash whenever possible. This means that, at first, she has to "make do" with lesser stuff. But she doesn't have compound interest working against her since she refuses to become someone else's asset. She too likes nice stuff but not enough to lose control over her money in order to get it. She prefers to think long term and work toward financial independence. Being financially free is more important to her than getting the best flat screen TV or the nicest car.

Over time an interesting thing happens in the lives of these two extreme examples. The "Now" person who buys nice stuff up front loses his buying power over time. Interest payments eat away at his spending power, he becomes more and more enslaved to his income source, and gradually over time he is able to acquire less and less nice stuff. As time passes, that nice stuff ages and breaks, and there are fewer and fewer dollars to repair or replace them. On the other hand, the "Later" person, free from the headwind of mounting debt payments, accumulates assets and spending power. As time goes by, she gains buying power. Further, her ability to delay gratification allows her to be choosier and wait until the right moment to buy nice stuff, meaning that she often gets it on sale.

The cumulative result is quite shocking. The person who dedicated himself so fervently to buying nice stuff ends up with mostly just junky stuff, while the person who made do with junky stuff early on quite quickly is able to acquire nothing but nice stuff. The two have switched positions entirely.

What's worse, the person who had to have nice stuff right away and got reduced by consumer debt is not prepared to weather any kind of financial storm. And know this: financial storms *always* come along. Nobody is immune from income interruptions, sicknesses, or even bad swings in the economy. Those who spend all their money and more are the ones left in the most peril when the harsh winds of economic change come to blow, while those who have delayed their gratification and are building up their YOU, Inc. Investment Hierarchy have reserves stashed away to help them make it through the tough times. After a few decades, the "Now" person is often financially destitute, while the "Later" person is quite well off.

So when we talk about getting out of debt and delaying your gratification a little bit, don't think that it's all drudgery and sacrifice. Don't picture getting out of debt as some painful chore. You would even be wrong to think of it as boring. Getting out of debt is in fact exhilarating, liberating, and, in a pretty short time, quite rewarding. It won't be long until you are acquiring the nice stuff but in the right way this time. If it sounds too good to be true, it almost is. But that's just the power inherent in compound interest. You either get on the destructive side of it or the productive side. The choice is up to you.

If you choose to place yourself firmly in the hands of the positive power of compounding, the rest of this book is for you.

THREE

Building Your Financial Life—A Complete Picture

"Hope is not a strategy."
—Anonymous

The story is told of three blind wise men each feeling a different part of an elephant. One shouted that it was long and slender, another that it was fat and bulbous, and the third that it was thin and floppy. From these localized descriptions, one might think that its trunk, its belly, or its ear represented the elephant. But for those of us with command of the complete picture, we know that each of the blind men was correct in his way, but none was looking at the whole truth. It was only when putting all three of their observations together that we got closer to describing the complexity of an actual elephant.

Finances have the tendency to fall prey to the same localized descriptions. Talk to a stockbroker, and to hear him tell it, investing is all about stocks. Talk to an insurance agent, and he'll focus you in on insurance and annuities. Talk to an estate planner, and she'll tell you all about wills and trusts. Listen to your benefits manager at work, and you might think the whole world of investing goes no further than your 401(k). Get with a real estate agent, and you'll be convinced that properties are the best investment.

All of these are correct in their way. But just as with the blind wise men describing the elephant, none of them presents the complete picture until they are put together.

When Benjamin Graham and Jason Zweig recommended putting together a comprehensive financial plan, we took it to mean piecing together all of these disparate parts so that we get the whole elephant. For us, we're going to be considering three different parts of the financial elephant and making sure to put them together so that you can craft for yourself a truly comprehensive financial plan. We think that as you live through your financial life, you will want to have your tax picture properly taken care of, your investments well allocated, and your insurances in place where they belong. To focus too much on one of these areas or to leave out others entirely is equally unwise. Let's consider these three different parts of your financial elephant.

Legal

Let's look at legal considerations as the first of the three parts of the elephant. Under the category of legal considerations for your financial plan, we must be sure to take a look at taxes. While you will need to get yourself a competent tax adviser for estate planning purposes and another expert at preparing your taxes, it will still be helpful here to take a broad survey of areas in which to be aware.

Unless you are extremely rare (and we're sure you are, but we mean financially), taxes will be the biggest expense you have to deal with in your lifetime. Properly handling taxes will be one of the most important things to do while building wealth. And let us give this warning: do not play around in this category. We have never understood people who get cute with their taxes, go delinquent on their payments or filings, or cheat. Sovereign governments are the most powerful entities on this earth, and to mess around with the money they demand of you is simply playing with fire. At the least, you will end up paying penalties, late fees, and interest (and possibly getting on their watch lists for future audits and scrutiny); at the worst, you could go to jail. So please do yourself a favor, and play the game totally straight when it comes to paying your taxes and abiding by all tax and inheritance laws. This is why it is so critical to get yourself both a good accountant and a good estate planner.

Let's talk about the accountant first. If your life is super simple and you have a very basic financial picture, it is probably okay for you to prepare your taxes yourself. But we still wouldn't recommend it. There are literally tens of thousands of pages of code in the tax laws of most countries in the developed world, and the taxpayer (you!) is responsible to follow every one of them! Thinking you are saving a few bucks by doing it yourself is really just naïve. You may want to go through the exercise of doing them yourself, just so you understand what your obligations really are, but then have it all checked out by a professional before filing. This is one category in which you don't want to scrimp.

Now, don't get us wrong. You shouldn't pay exorbitant fees for getting your taxes prepared, but you should spend the money necessary to have them done correctly and on time. Also, the larger your income and the more complicated your different streams of income and list of assets becomes, the more you are going to want an accountant/bookkeeper that you pay monthly. You might be surprised at how affordable this is, and a little bit of money for a competent professional can go a long way toward giving you peace of mind that things are being done correctly.

Here is the principle. You get paid to do what you do. And theoretically, the better you do it and/or the more you do it, the better you will be compensated. This means that you need to focus on what you do that brings in the bacon so that you can bring in even more. You are the goose that lays the golden eggs, so be sure to focus on laying those eggs. (Okay, too many farm analogies here.) In all seriousness, you need to focus in on the main ways you contribute to your cash flow. Anything you do to divert or distract your focus from that is diminishing your earning potential. Therefore, let someone else do your bookkeeping and accounting so you can focus on doing what you do best.

When it comes to taxes, many deductions are available to business owners that are not available to employees. What this means is that those compensated (in the United States) on a 1099 basis file their taxes a little differently than do those who are paid a wage and are compensated on a W2 basis. Generally speaking, the 1099 recipient gets to declare her expenses and deduct those expenses from the amount she owes before paying in that amount (when the incomes get high enough, this occurs monthly and then weekly). The W2 wage earner has her taxes taken out each paycheck and then files a return at the end of the year, at which point she is limited to a handful of basic itemized deductions such as mortgage interest, dependents, and charitable contributions. This is one reason we encourage people to consider going into business for themselves.

Many tax laws are frankly favorable to the small business owner because the government realizes how important those businesses are to the economy. For example, small businesses in the United States account for 55 percent of all the jobs. The government is very interested in small businesses continuing to supply those jobs, so it provides legal deductions to help small businesses prosper. Again, consult a certified public accountant (CPA) for your specific situation.

Another enormous consideration when it comes to building your wealth, especially for the long term, is estate planning. This means crafting how your assets are held so that they pass along to your designated beneficiaries in the most tax-efficient way when you die. What does this mean in plain language? It means if you just die and leave a bunch of money lying around, much of it will go to the government because you didn't properly "get your affairs in order." Believe it or not, the governments of most developed nations take a big share of your assets when you die, unless you have them prearranged in legal ways that minimize such "death taxes."

Now, if you don't have many assets to speak of, this is not much of a worry just yet. But once you know what's in this book and learn about some of the insurance products you should probably utilize, there *will* be assets to be passed on when you die. No matter your age, it is never too early to begin understanding these concepts.

The simplest and quickest step to take, which can be done for a few hundred bucks (and online for free, though we don't recommend it), is to have a simple *Will and Testament* prepared. The Creighton Law Offices define a Will and Testament as "the legal document by which you identify those individuals (or charities) that are to receive your property and possessions on your death. These individuals and charities are commonly referred to as the beneficiaries under your last will and testament." Having this simple document prepared now and filed with a law firm or at least in a safe place is an extremely good idea. If you should die, your loved ones will be distraught (at least you should hope so). In their grief, they don't need to be left to figure out what you intended for your possessions once you were gone. And in their grief, they may even be cheered by receiving some of your money instead of having to instead hand much of it to the government. In your Will and Testament you can specify whom you would like to receive specific nostalgic items or heirlooms. Do your family a favor and get this prepared.

Along with the Will and Testament is usually a document called a *Durable Power of Attorney*. This is necessary if you ever became mentally incapacitated. A durable power of attorney basically means that the document takes over if you are incapacitated and unable to make decisions on your own. It specifies a person you name who will be legally designated to take care of important decisions for you. This could involve paying your bills, handling your assets, and taking charge of your medical care. If something should happen to you in the absence of such documents, your loved ones (again, in their grief) will have to actually go to court to get the power to handle these affairs for you. In many cases this document is actually two: one for your finances and one for your medical care (including your wishes regarding life-sustaining treatment and other such controversial decisions you don't want to inflict upon your loved ones). Setting up these documents is child's play for any competent professional, and the costs are really low compared to all the stress and hassle you will potentially be saving your loved ones down the road. Be sure to make the preparation of these documents a part of your overall financial plan.

As you put together your Comprehensive Financial Plan, a final legal consideration is the taxability of different types of investments. Because even small costs make enormous differences over time, it is very important to keep taxes in mind when making long-term investments. We will cover specifics in chapters 6 and 7, but as a general principle, making an investment without first considering the tax implications could cost you a lot (and we emphasize: a *lot*) of money. Again, this is another reason why it is important to have an expert you can consult before making any moves that may have tax consequences (either on the front end, when you are beginning an investment, or on the back end, when you are liquidating one).

Insurance

A second part of the elephant to understand is insurance. Of course, there are many types of insurances, from auto to home to liability policies. But we will restrict ourselves to discussing only those that should properly be considered as part of your Comprehensive Financial Plan. Still, an overriding principle is that insurance is necessary to protect you from calamity. Again, we are stunned to learn of people who drive around without car insurance, or live in a home without a policy on it. There is no excuse for putting yourself at such risk. People who do are playing Russian roulette with their financial futures. Don't ever be so reckless. Get insurance to properly protect you and your family from catastrophe.

We understand that insurance can seem expensive and that making those payments can be painful, but one emergency is all it takes for a lifetime of thankfulness that insurance coverage was in place. Make sure you are covered for medical emergencies, disability, critical illness, and other possibilities that could have a huge impact on your ability or willingness to continue bringing in income. Protect your homes and cars as prudent. And the more you have to lose, the more you'll want to be sure to have umbrella policies in place insuring you against liability. Again, consult an expert (or several) to figure out what is best for your particular situation. But don't leave this area unexamined.

Another aspect of insurance to think about is life insurance. It seems there aren't many categories as misunderstood or maligned as life insurance. Some of the things we hear said are incredible. Life insurance is not only a really good idea for protecting your loved ones against economic hardship in the instance of your passing, but it can also become a great wealth-building investment and a key part of your Comprehensive Financial Plan.

There are basically two types of life insurance: term and permanent. *Term* life insurance works like this: you pay a monthly or annual premium (an amount of money you lose forever) for the right of your beneficiaries (those you designate) to receive a lump sum of money when you die. It's that simple. When you are young and in good health, this type of insurance is very cheap, meaning, the premium payments are low. Hundreds of thousands of dollars' worth of coverage (the amount that will be paid out to your beneficiaries upon your death) can be had for a few hundred bucks a year. There is really no excuse for any income earner with dependents (a spouse and/or kids) not to have at least this very basic type of life insurance in place. If you were to die suddenly without this, would your dependents be able to continue on without your income? Would they be able to hold the memorial services and pay for the burial or cremation (or funeral pyre or burning barge, take your pick)? We have seen fathers unexpectedly leave behind young families without this simple protection. Don't let that happen to you. Contact a competent insurance provider, and get a simple term policy to at least cover the worst case if it should happen.

The second major type of life insurance is *permanent* insurance. In this category there are really three main divisions: whole life, universal life, and index universal life. These products provide death benefit coverage, as does the term insurance just described, but with an added twist: they also accumulate what's called a cash balance as the years go along. As you continue to pay in premiums over the years, your cash value grows tax free (at least in the United States at the time of this writing). In most cases, your death benefit also grows. Keep making the premium payments each year (or month), and these two balances grow and grow and grow. This cash is yours. You can take it out at any time. But doing so will have an impact on your death benefit with the policy and will incur a tax hit (you'll have to pay taxes on the gains in the cash balance that occurred over the years). A superior approach to getting your hands on that money is to "borrow" it from yourself. You can then use this money tax free, as it is a loan and not a removal of the funds. In most of these policies the full cash amount continues to grow as if the entire principal were still in place, even when you have some of the money out on loan to yourself![1] Study these products a little bit and you will see why some call this strategy, "becoming your own banker." The concept is that if you are going to need to borrow money once in a while over the course of your life, you may as well borrow it from yourself. Why use someone else's money when you can use your own?

Whole Life has a fixed ratio between its cash value and its death benefit. Universal Life allows some modification to optimize either the cash value or the death benefit.

An Index Universal Life (IUL) insurance policy is one whose cash value grows by mimicking the performance of an index. We'll cover indices later in some depth, but the point is that they are collections of securities designed to represent a portion of a market. For instance, the Dow Jones Industrial Average is an index, comprised of the top thirty largest company stocks being traded on the NY Stock Exchange. If that collection of thirty stocks goes up 1 percent on a given day, the "Dow" is said to have gone up 1 percent. This is how an index works. It's simply a collection of securities lumped together for shorthand representative measuring of market performance.

In the case of an Index Universal Life Insurance product, the growth of its cash value is tied to the performance of an index (without actually being invested directly in the index). In some of these products, the insurer will guarantee you that your cash value will never go down (providing you a floor of zero percent) but will credit you the upside growth of a certain index (either capped at a certain percentage or at least keeping a small percent for the insurance company). Some of them will even go further and guarantee you a minimum growth percentage after looking back over, say, three years. If the three-year rearward review

---

1 This is because the money withdrawn for the loan comes from the insurance company with your cash balance as collateral.

shows that you earned less than a certain amount, they'll go back and credit you enough cash to bring you up to their guaranteed minimum percentage. It is a nice setup because it's got growth potential on the upside with a guaranteed floor on the downside.

Example time. Let's say you own an IUL policy tied to the S&P 500 Index (another of the most popular stock market indices), which goes up 12 percent this year. Let's also say that your policy states that you get all but 1.5 percent of the index's gain each year. So in this case the cash value in your policy would grow by a tax-free interest amount of 10.5 percent this year. Not too shabby. But let's say next year the S&P 500 goes *down* 6 percent. What happens to your cash value? In most IUL policies today, you would be guaranteed a floor of zero percent, so your cash value would be safe and wouldn't go down at all. And then, as we stated, many of these policies do a backward look after three years or so to make sure your cash grows by at least some minimum, in this case let's say 3 percent (these terms are all stated in the policy). So if the S&P 500 went down into negative territory for three years in a row (which almost never happens), after those three years your insurance policy would credit to your cash balance the amount necessary to get you up to their minimum guaranteed growth of at least 3 percent annually. As this very typical example demonstrates, you get most of the upside potential of market growth with *none* of the downside risk!

So why do some people think permanent life insurance is a bad deal? We're not sure, actually. Sometimes you'll hear that it seems too complicated and therefore can't be good. Most often, however, you will hear that it's expensive and it only enriches the agent selling the policy. Sure, you are paying much higher premiums than you would if you were merely buying term insurance. But permanent life insurance is just that—*permanent*. When you get older and your health declines, you've got the policy in place and it's guaranteed for life (after a certain point) to pay your death benefit even when you're done paying in premiums. Term insurance, on the other hand, is usually only good for about twenty-five years (this length of time is clearly stated when you buy it). Once that term runs out, the insurance company is through covering you, and all the premiums you've paid are gone forever. There is no cash balance and no continuation of the death benefit. The other problem in such cases is that now you're older, your health may be fading, and buying additional term insurance will now be super expensive, if even possible with your health conditions.

Permanent life insurance also plays nicely into estate planning. This is especially true if the death benefits are large enough that they make it possible for your surviving loved ones to pay the estate taxes on your assets without having to sell off many of them. If the death benefit is not needed for this purpose upon your death, it can then be distributed among your heirs and/or bequeathed to charity. These options are all nice to have in place, especially if you are planning on going *beyond* financial fitness. (Of course, term insurance can also be used in these ways upon death, but only if you happen to die at a young enough age that your term policy is still in effect.)

One of the shortcuts to wealth is to see what the wealthy do and copy them. And something you will see again and again among the wealthy (and even in large corporations) is the use of permanent life insurance as a long-term investment strategy. For this reason alone, you should seek a competent adviser and investigate whether it makes sense for your particular case. (It's probably best to get more than one insurance representative and have them compete against each other for your business. To give the critics of this type of insurance their due, there *are* a lot of ways these policies can be gold mines for the agents selling them, and by making them compete, you will be sure to get the best deal.) If you are young and don't yet make much money, simple term insurance is probably where you should start. But as soon as you can get it cranking, talk to a professional about beginning the wealth accumulation that a permanent life insurance policy provides. In many instances, even a combination of term and permanent life insurance is a good idea.

As author and life insurance expert Jake Thompson wrote, "Money inside cash value life insurance, when handled properly, grows tax free, can be used tax free, and passes on tax free." Those reasons should be enough for anyone serious about going beyond financial fitness to see if it is right for their Comprehensive Financial Plan.

Financial

The final part of the elephant to consider is the financial. This is the belly, the largest portion of the beast, to be sure. Much of the rest of the book will examine the various financial aspects you should consider in structuring your Comprehensive Financial Plan, so we'll confine ourselves here to *retirement planning*.

Retirement is a relatively new invention in human history. Nowhere in ancient literature do we catch even a glimpse of elderly people rocking in leisure chairs or golfing in Florida. Throughout history people have stayed more or less gainfully employed right up until the bitter end. Admittedly, part of the reason for that was because their bitter end came around at a time closer to what we would call our bitter middle! That's because life expectancies have increased greatly with modern medicine and the like. But culturally, the idea of quitting one's vocation and taking up full-time play never even entered the minds of our forebears. We say all this because we want you to seriously consider whether you really want to retire.

Warren Buffett, whom we've mentioned before, is certainly "of retirement age" (whatever that means). But he's still going strong, managing one of the world's largest fortunes and apparently loving every minute of it (and who could blame him?). We could give countless other examples. In fact, continuing to do meaningful work on a daily basis, to have somewhere to go, and to have others to interact with, have all been proven to be healthy for us both mentally and physiologically. So, in effect, working longer can help us actually live longer. So just because it's become some kind of a cultural norm, don't think that you are obligated to retire like everybody else. Go ahead and do what you love all the way to the end, if your heart desires it!

You can probably tell that we don't necessarily like this culture of removing some of the most distinguished, experienced, and wise contributors from our society and casting them off to the shuffleboard parks. We think that if some people want to keep jamming right along, society's expectations shouldn't stop them from doing so.

With that said, however, we *do* understand that not everyone loves what they do. For sure, many people are just not blessed with the kind of health to continue working into advanced years. And unfortunately, none of us has a crystal ball, and we can't be sure what we'll want for ourselves that far down the road—or even what we'll be able to do. Therefore, "retirement planning" seems like a good safety factor even if you choose not to use it in the conventional way when you get there.

The other side of the coin, also, is people who don't wish to wait until they are "of age" in order to retire. Some people are happy enough with their current employment, but in no way do they wish to do it long term. They instead have their eye on a lifelong dream, something they deeply wish to do once they can get money to be no object. For this group of people who (in a sense) wish to "retire early," the need for proper planning is even more urgent.

So just what does it mean to prepare for retirement, and how does one go about it? This is a many-sided question. If you're following the overall theme of this book, you won't be surprised to learn that the macro process of accumulating assets and going *beyond* financial fitness is the main strategy. That's it in a general sense: acquire enough assets that generate cash flow, so that when you choose to retire (early, when you are "of age," or whenever), your passive income from those assets will be enough to pay for your lifestyle. Easy enough, right?

We think it might now be getting obvious why we're so intent on putting the power of compound interest to work *for* you rather than *against* you. This is because of the tremendous power of compounding to build small contributions, over time, into large sums. This, in most cases, is what you will need to do in order to properly plan for retirement.

You will need to accumulate enough assets, but how much is enough? It all depends upon the person, of course, but many financial advisers recommend targeting at least twenty times the amount in principle that you will need to live off of each year. That means that if you think you'll need $50,000 per year, your targeted principal amount of assets you'll be drawing from should be at least $1 million. This may be a good rule of thumb, but for many reasons, it may also be low. We believe you should shoot for the high side just to be safe. What if you said twenty-five or thirty times your annual need?

Such numbers may seem impossible to you right now reading this. That's okay. We understand. But this book is all about making those kinds of numbers a reality. By learning financial literacy now, you can begin applying it directly to your future. We believe that you will never regret a moment spent making your future life easier for yourself. In fact, we believe that if it were possible, your future self would come back in time and give your present self a big old hug for doing so.

As you consider the total amount you will want for your nest egg, remember that you will build that up through a variety of investments. If you build up a business, that business is an asset (maybe your biggest one) and can be sold or lived off of when the time is right for you to do so. Having permanent life insurance, as we just discussed, can be a big part of your assets too, enabling you to borrow from it each year to help meet your annual spending needs. But you need to learn about many additional vehicles, all of which can be part of your growing total asset collection or what many refer to as your "portfolio." And as we'll see, one of the keys to assembling a proper portfolio is diversification across a broad range of asset classes and investment tools. To begin reviewing each of these and how they fit together, it's time to dig into what Benjamin Graham calls your Investment Policy.

CHAPTER 3 ACTION LIST

1. **Find an accountant to file your taxes for you and (if applicable), keep your books for you on an ongoing basis.**
2. **Hire a lawyer or legal service to prepare your Will and Testament and Durable Power of Attorney documents.**
3. **Have an initial conversation with an Estate Planner and see if there are steps you should be taking in this category.**
4. **Think about and investigate whether or not starting a business of your own might be right for you.**
5. **Make sure you have the following insurances in place: home, flood, car, medical, disability, critical illness, extended care, and an umbrella liability policy.**
6. **Consult a professional to either review or initiate life insurance policies appropriate for your situation.**
7. **Determine the amount of money you'd like to have coming in each year in "retirement" and set 20 to 30 times that amount as your target principle amount.**

PART II

INVESTMENT POLICY

SPELLING OUT YOUR FUNDAMENTAL
APPROACH TO INVESTING

FOUR

The Top of the Hierarchy

"The great majority of people do not build up any wealth because they do not practice the self-discipline of saving some of their income every month."
—Sir John Templeton

Now that you have at least conceived your Comprehensive Financial Plan, you've determined to accumulate assets that generate cash flow over time, and you've further looked across the whole landscape of financial preparation including insurance, legal, and tax considerations, it's time to begin developing your Investment Policy. This is where you will determine exactly how your money will flow from your efforts to your assets.

> It's time to begin developing your Investment Policy. This is where you will determine exactly how your money will flow from your efforts to your assets.

Let's revisit the water pump illustration. As you turn the crank to earn your income (and even add additional cranks through the ownership of a business, or what Robert Kiyosaki would call earning money from more than one quadrant), you will be flowing portions of that income into the YOU, Inc. Investment Hierarchy. Remember that you will be starting at the bottom and working your way up, always investing in yourself as you go. You will find, we believe, that in a relatively short time after getting out of debt, you will build your emergency fund and complete your survival preparation. Money will then begin flowing into level 4, savings. At this point, it is time to take a look at the other levels of the YOU, Inc. Hierarchy and begin thinking about a strategy for flowing income into these various asset levels.

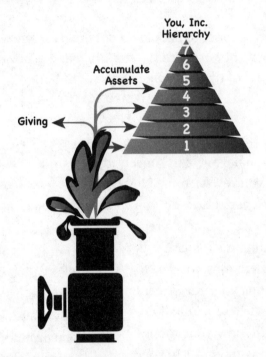

The bottom levels of the YOU, Inc. hierarchy are the largest because they are the most important. They are also, roughly speaking, the *safest*. The higher you ascend the hierarchy, the riskier your investments are.

Risk is an interesting term. Almost everyone has a pretty good intrinsic understanding of what it means, but precise definitions are a bit more difficult. Economists are divided over the relationship between risk and reward. Many say that the higher the risk, the higher the potential reward. But value investors like War-ren Buffett and Benjamin Graham very clearly state that the best deals (and therefore the highest rewards) can often be found in investments that are the best bargains and therefore the least risky.

Leaving these professional squabbles to the side, the generally accepted concept of risk versus reward is what we are trying to demonstrate with the YOU, Inc. Hierarchy. The idea is that level 4 investments are riskier than level 3 investments. Again, this is a very general relationship and can't be strictly true for every type of investment we'll explore, but in a broad sense we are simply trying to steer you through safe territory before ratcheting up the risk.

It might be more accurate to state that the higher one goes on the YOU, Inc. Hierarchy, the more *sophisticated* the investments get, and the less things are under your direct control. This is inar-guably true. The higher one proceeds, the more one must know or else risk getting burned either by ignorance, hucksters, market forces, or all three!

Also, since sophistication rises as you proceed upward on the hierarchy, *complication* rises as well. This means that it becomes more and more important to seek competent advice as you go higher. Now, if it is your profession, say, to manage money for a hedge fund, then investing in some of the securities we put at the top of the hierarchy is no big deal to you. Obviously, experts in these fields are not at the same level of risk as the rest of us who are merely ascending this scale in order to properly structure our personal portfolios of assets. So in general, for the average per-son seeking to go beyond financial fitness, the higher you climb on the hierarchy, the more you need to know about what you're doing, and the more you should realize the potential, or at least possibility, of losing some or all of your assets at those levels.

Don't let this scare you off. There are wonderful investments on these higher levels of the hierarchy. And knowing about them, what makes them work, and how they should be arranged relative to all your other assets is going to insulate you against the possibilities of loss. So by all means, proceed upward, but do so with proper information and guidance.

Not everyone takes this careful approach of ascending upward into risk gradually, just as not everyone works on physical fitness before attempting to build muscle. It would be futile to build strong biceps if you weren't at the same time working to slim down your overall physique (picture big biceps and a pot belly). In the same way, it is futile to jump in at the top of the hierarchy and try to "strike it rich." We have actually known people with this gambler's mentality. Buried in consumer debt, they try to leap past the disciplines of getting out of debt and building assets from the bottom up; instead, they plow into something like day-trading tech stocks. We don't have to tell you how things ended up in every one of these cases we've observed.

In a nutshell, there is no real shortcut to financial independence (and even when there appears to be, as in winning the lottery, it never seems to last, as the person who received money unearned only seems to squander it quickly). Just as a journey of a thousand miles begins with a single step and proceeds step by step from there, so too does one accumulate assets that generate cash flow and eventually deliver financial freedom. It takes time, it takes a disciplined approach, and it requires patience and perseverance. But truly the tortoise wins the race here, in almost every instance.

Just what are those remaining levels on the hierarchy? Level 5 is CDs, money market accounts, and most types of bonds. Level 6 is stocks and real estate. Finally, level 7 is speculative ventures, start-ups, and inventions. Actually, there are many more investment types at each of these levels. We will explore these in detail in chapters 6 and 7. The rest of this book is really about these final three levels of the YOU, Inc. Hierarchy. So you'll have your fill of these vehicles and many more by the time we're done.

Long-Term Value Investing

We've mentioned a couple of times now the term *value investing*. Strictly speaking, this is the strategy of finding bargains (meaning high value) in the various investment classes out there and buying them and holding them for the long term. The highest profile examples of this are Benjamin Graham and Warren Buffett. Experts at security analysis, they understand (or understood) the numbers of a business's balance sheet better than anyone. They are (or were) extremely adept at finding hidden gems of value where others didn't think to look and then making courageous investments on a large scale in those bargains. One such investment by Graham consumed 25 percent of his already massive portfolio at the time, but it grew to be worth an enormous sum over the ensuing years. Finding value at a low price based on corporate financial fundamentals, buying in heavy, and then holding for the extreme long-term is the essence of value investing.

> Finding value at a low price based on corporate financial fundamentals, buying in heavy, and then holding for the extreme long-term is the essence of value investing.

Although most of the rest of us will never be anywhere near the Grahams or Buffetts of the world when it comes to security analysis and stock picking, we *can* copy their long-term buy-and-hold strategy. As for finding bargains, that is still largely the domain of professionals who have the time and expertise to apply to that task. Unless you are going to make it your profession, thinking you can do in your spare time what experts have enough trouble doing full-time is a silly notion. But there are ways to smooth things out and model some of their behaviors, and most of the world's experts are pretty free with their advice about what might be good for the rest of us. We'll discuss these in more detail when we cover index investing.

For now, the lesson to take from these titans of value investing is that buying quality and holding it for the long term can produce enormous returns. There are several reasons for this. One is the tremendous power of compounding we've already covered many times in these pages. Another is the cost of buying and selling most paper assets. Usually, brokerage fees for "trading" stocks and bonds and other securities can quickly eat into your long-term profits. Also, brokerage houses make money on the "spread" (the difference between the *bid* and the *ask,* or what people are willing to sell a security for and what others are willing to pay to buy it); consumers often know nothing about this house profit but pay it anyway.

Buying and selling also create tax obligations that can sometimes obliterate any financial gains in a transaction. For the long-term investor, however, the capital gains are not taxed until they are *realized*—that is, until the asset is actually sold. Simply holding a security that has gone up in price doesn't incur any capital gains tax obligation, and brokerages earn no fees for merely holding on to securities over time. So by holding on to investments for the long term, one dodges fees and taxes and preserves the power of compounding.

Efficient Market Hypothesis (EMH)

Another reason the long-term buy-and-hold strategy is a good one for most paper securities traded on the open market is something called the *efficient market hypothesis (EMH).* This simply states that all of the important information about a stock or bond is already contained in its price. Do you think that Tesla stock will go up in the future because of a new car model announcement coming up? Think again. The market knows about that announcement and has already factored that increase into the price—or so the theory goes.

Those who adhere to this belief maintain that the market and its movements are therefore basically random. Since all information is already baked into the price of securities by the hordes of piranhas circling to eat up any deals, nobody can really predict whether a security (or a commodity) will "go up" or "go down." Therefore, price movements are totally random. This means that no one can actually "beat" the market. As John Bogle, former CEO and founder of the Vanguard Group, one of the world's largest mutual fund companies and the pioneer in index investing, likes to quote a friend of his who was a stock runner one summer: "I'm going to tell you everything you need to know about the stock market: nobody knows nothin.'"

Interestingly, a lot of data seems to support this. Study after study shows that even the so-called experts who run mutual funds and hedge funds often don't outperform the market indices, such as the S&P 500 or the Dow Jones Industrial Average we spoke about before. What this means is that investing in a basket of stocks in proportion to their standing in an index (most easily done through an *index* mutual fund or exchange-traded fund, which we'll cover later) will give you a higher return than handing your money to a professional money manager. Even the high fliers who *do* manage to beat the market (only some 4 percent of fund managers do in any given year, by the way) rarely repeat that performance the next year! This means that even if you did get fortunate (lucky) enough to entrust your money to a professional manager who is able to beat the market in year one, there is very little chance that he or she will duplicate the feat in year two (or any later year).

Now, there are some enormous exceptions to this, such as the original hedge fund manager A. W. Jones, Julian Robertson's Tiger Fund, George Soros's and Jim Rogers' Quantum Fund, Peter Lynch's famous decade-and-a-half run of beating the market, the ongoing returns of James Simon's Medallion Fund at Renaissance Technologies, or the consistently high performance of Ken Griffin's Citadel. But these are truly the exceptions to the rule, and they are either long gone or closed to outside investors like you. For the most part, the "professional" money managers and mutual fund captains who charge you to try to beat the market with your money fall hopelessly short of the mark.

These facts should disabuse you of any notion that you can throw some money in the markets and outfox everyone else there. It simply would not happen. What would happen, however, is that you would lose your money. If by some chance you didn't, it would only embolden you to go back again and again until you finally *did* lose your money. Quickly or gradually, the result would be the same. Trust us, the statistics don't lie. If professionals require sophisticated computer systems, real-time ticker information, direct connections to prime brokers, sophisticated arbitrage strategies, and armies of analysts to even come close to "beating the market," unless you dedicate your life to becoming one of them and learning what they know so you too can do what they do, you are wasting not only your money but also your time.

Index Investing

Therefore, one of the best strategies to at least consider for the long-term building of your portfolio is index investing. As stated, this concept basically involves buying into a basket of stocks or bonds (or several other asset classes) in proportion to some recognized index (of which there are many). If the fund follows the S&P 500 index, for instance, it would own the same companies represented in the index in the same proportion in which they are in relation to the other companies on the index. There is no "active" trading or attempting to beat the market. Not only does this approach almost always outrun those who try to beat the market, as we've already discussed, but it also incurs less expense because very little trading is taking place. The resulting brokerage fees are much smaller and the tax implications even smaller. For this reason, index funds (either mutual funds or exchange traded funds, to be explained in chapter 6) are the most cost-effective funds an average investor can buy into. Remember how important low costs are over time when considering the exponential growth of an investment. This advantage to index investing is not insubstantial.

Jason Zweig wrote, "Recognize that an index fund—which owns all the stocks in the market, all the time, without any pretense of being able to select the 'best' and avoid the 'worst'—will beat most funds over the long run. It's rock-bottom overhead . . . [giving] the index fund an insurmountable advantage . . . . [As] the years pass, the cost advantage of indexing will keep accruing relentlessly. Hold an index fund for 20 years or more, adding new money every month, and you are all but certain to outperform the vast majority of professional and individual investors alike." This is almost too good to be true! But there it is in black and white, directly from one of the world's experts on investing.

Dollar Cost Averaging

Zweig indicated something very important in that quote: "adding new money every month." This concept is known as *dollar cost averaging*, and along with long-term value investing into index funds, it is one of the most important strategies for the individual investor.

Here is how it works.

Remember when we talked about "paying yourself first"? We said to set things up so that your deposits into your emergency fund or savings occur automatically. Then we recommended that you establish your charitable contributions in a similar automatic manner. It's the same principle here. You are much more likely to accomplish something over the long term when you put systems in place to make it automatic, simple, and easy. Otherwise you won't stick with it. Sure, right now reading this book, you may be getting pretty fired up about your finances. Maybe you're motivated enough to dig out your checkbook and send off some money to an index fund (please don't do that yet; we've got a lot to cover with you first). But over time, as the excitement of this book fades (alas, as all good things are fleeting), you will want to have systems in place to turn your good intentions into systematic actions. This is one of the signs of maturity: the ability to turn impulse into habit. This is best facilitated through automation. This is what dollar cost averaging accomplishes: it puts your ongoing investments on autopilot.

But that is not its only advantage.

Dollar cost averaging also takes all the guesswork and timing out of your purchases in the market. You don't have to listen to all the financial chatter on the cable television programs (although you might want to if you'd like to learn some complicated terms to help you sound smart at a party). You don't need to scour the pages of the *Wall Street Journal*. John Bogle says to ignore those things anyway. Instead, you will be buying into the market consistently through all seasons, good and bad. You will catch highs in the market, but you will also be purchasing during lows. And the

> "You will automatically be going in harder when things are on sale and lighter when they are pricey."
> —Jason Zweig

interesting thing is, since you will be putting in the same amount each month, when your money goes to buy stocks or bonds or funds or whatever, if the market is up, your money will buy less of them. When the market is down, your money will buy more of them. You will automatically be going in harder when things are on sale and lighter when they are pricey. It's all on autopilot, and it seems almost like magic!

We know someone who has bought gold this way since 2002, beginning back when it was selling for approximately $300 an ounce. Over the years she just kept buying. Sometimes the price was up; sometimes it was down. Overall through those years, gold trended upward. But because of her dollar cost averaging approach, she didn't worry too much about the price of gold at any given time. She just bought it consistently on a regular basis. And today, when gold is trading in a historically high range, her basis (the amount of money she's got invested) is way below the value of her investment. She was able to do this stress free, with very little time expended, almost automatically. That's the power of dollar cost averaging, and it's a tremendous strategy for the individual investor.

Your Investment Policy

Again, as always, seek advice for your particular situation. We cannot know all the intricacies of your finances or your specific goals. Our desire is to educate you in financial literacy so you can go beyond financial fitness. It is our hope that you will consider each of these strategies and make them fit your needs as you determine best.

Let's review what we've covered in this chapter in terms of putting together your investment policy. First of all, you know that your goal is to accumulate assets. The strategy we have discussed involves flowing income from your money pump into the

YOU, Inc. Investment Hierarchy, working from the bottom up. In such a way you will be easing into more sophisticated investments and taking on increased risk in gradual steps. Realizing that it is futile to try and cheat your way forward by attempting to "beat the market," you will take a long-term view and buy value over time. This can most easily be done by investing in index funds, and this in turn can be put on a type of autopilot through the technique called dollar cost averaging.

On to the next.

FIVE

Risk Factors Working Against You

"There are really two Americas, one for the grifter class, and one for everybody else. In everybody-else land, the world of small businesses and wage-earning employees, the government is something to be avoided, an overwhelming, all-powerful entity whose attentions usually presage some kind of financial setback, if not complete ruin. In the grifter world, however, government is a slavish lapdog that the financial companies . . . use as a tool for making money."
—MATT TAIBBI, *GRIFTOPIA*

It will be helpful to know that things are rigged, and they are not rigged in your favor. You are a little guppy in a big pond and forced to play by the rules—lots and lots of rules—even though not everyone plays by the same set of rules. These rules, and the truths that surround them, are the headwinds working against your forward progress.

In the original *Financial Fitness* book we talked about the three aspects of money: defense, offense, and the playing field. The *playing field* represented the external financial environment in which we all must operate. If money were a game, the playing field would represent the rules of that game, its weather, the playing conditions, the impartiality (or otherwise) of the referees, and everything that surrounds or impacts that game. Financially speaking, the playing field includes many factors we must be aware of in order to maximize the effectiveness of our asset accumulation and truly move beyond financial fitness. In this chapter, we're going to drill down deeper into the factors that oppose your financial efforts and/or put them at risk.

Remember that the higher you go up the YOU, Inc. Investment Hierarchy, in general, the more risk you take on. This means that it becomes increasingly important to take these factors into account as you grow your finances.

Interest Rates

One of the biggest risk factors to be aware of as you climb the YOU, Inc. Hierarchy is interest rates. These pesky numbers seem to sneak into just about any asset's valuation. The interest rate at any given moment has a direct bearing on the value of bonds, for instance, and a nearly direct impact on residential property values, to name just two. But the *movement* of interest rates also has its effects on the markets. For instance, when interest rates *rise*, bond prices go down. Who would want to pay you for an old bond with a lower rate when new bonds are being issued at the same face value for a higher rate? Therefore, the market price of the bonds you are holding decreases until the resulting yield comes into line with the new bonds. If at the time of an interest rate increase you happen to be the owner of some bonds, you just lost value. Of course, the opposite is true as well. It's that direct.

If interest rates get really high, savings accounts and simple interest–bearing investments become pretty good deals (because they are then paying high interest on deposits). When interest rates go very low (as they are at the time of this writing), people are basically discouraged from saving and are encouraged by the low rates to borrow "easy money" instead. Bubble conditions result as that easy money flows into the various markets.

This can all get pretty complicated quite quickly, so we won't go into much detail here, but just know that interest rates have a huge impact on the value of your assets. Never fear, as there are ways to protect yourself against this, which we'll discuss in chapter 8.

So how do interest rates get set? Who controls them, and why?

In the United States a central banking system called the Federal Reserve controls interest rates. The "Fed" is a private banking consortium originally established by edict of the US government and assigned the responsibility of managing the money supply of the United States. This is primarily accomplished through the following three mechanisms:

Open Market Operations – This is where the Fed either buys or sells US Treasury and/or US Federal Agency Bonds. When the Fed sells bonds, it takes in money, thereby "tightening" the money supply, meaning there is less of it in circulation. This results in an interest rate *rise*, because there is less money available for loans by commercial banks (those who take your deposits *in* and turn around and loan money *out*), and therefore those commercial banks have to charge a higher interest rate on loans just to make the same amount of overall profit.

Conversely, when the Fed purchases bonds, it disburses money, thereby "loosening" the money supply, meaning there is more of it in circulation. This results in an interest rate *decrease*, because there is more money for the banks to lend. Therefore they can charge a lower interest rate for doing so and make the same amount of overall profit.

Discount Rate – This is the interest rate that commercial banks must pay for government loans. The more the banks have to pay to get the money, the more they tend to charge to lend it back out again, and therefore interest rates rise. Conversely, the less the banks have to pay, the less they tend to charge, and therefore interest rates decline.

Reserve (or Margin) Requirements – This is the amount of money commercial banks are required to keep on hand in proportion to the amount of money they have out on loans. The higher the reserve required, the harder it is for the banks to make money by lending, so the interest rate they charge rises. The lower the reserve required, the more money they have available to lend, so the interest rate they must charge can go lower.

The reason we provided you with these explanations is to make it abundantly clear that someone is tampering with the value of your assets. This is one reason we will talk later about some of the investments you can make that are "tamperproof."

Inflation (and Deflation)

Closely related to interest rates are *inflation* and *deflation*, which are conditions that refer to the purchasing power of money as a result of the amount that is in circulation. When a significant supply of money flows into the economy (as for example when the Fed buys bonds), it tends to drive down the buying power of the dollars you already hold. This is because there are now more dollars in circulation fighting to buy the same finite amount of items. As a result, the price of those items tends to rise to match the new level of money available to buy them. It takes a little time for prices to rise once the new money flows into the economy, but this is what happens.

Do not confuse this with price increases that occur because of changes in supply and demand. Supply-and-demand price changes reflect the scarcity or abundance of something, such as the Ford Mustang prices when soldiers were first coming back to the United States from the Vietnam War in the late 1960s. There were so many young men who wanted that car that the demand drove the price way up. People were buying them straight off the lot for something like three thousand dollars, then turning around and selling them for a profit of a thousand dollars or more. This is a supply-and-demand effect on prices. It is not inflation. Remember, inflation and deflation occur when the *money supply* changes significantly. Supply-and-demand prices change when the *amount of goods and services* changes significantly.

Why is inflation (or its opposite, deflation) important? Because it directly affects the purchasing power of your money. Under conditions of inflation, your money gradually is able to buy less and less. Since a little bit of steady inflation is what the Federal Reserve shoots for (we'll get to the reason in a moment), your money continually shrinks in value. If inflation gets out of control and runs rampant (as happened in Germany under the Weimar Republic before Hitler and in Zimbabwe more recently), your US currency won't just be worth less, it could become *worthless*! Of course, that would be extreme, and the Federal Reserve watches this closely and attempts to tweak interest rates to keep it "under control."

What exactly do they do? By using the three mechanisms described above, they raise interest rates to slow down inflation, and they decrease interest rates to reduce deflation.

Of the two, people are usually more afraid of deflation. Deflation is simply the condition in which prices drop because there is less money in circulation to buy the same amount of goods. Although a drop in prices sounds really good to anyone with money, what generally happens with deflation is panic for those who do *not* have money (and especially for those who are in debt). Money becomes scarce, and people freak out. Let's use oxygen as an analogy. When there is an abundance of oxygen (inflation), you may hardly even notice it. You may feel a bit stronger or more energetic, or may sleep better, but you don't really notice it much. But if oxygen became scarce (deflation), people would start to suffocate, causing intense panic.

Many experts agree that this is what happened during the Great Depression. Much of the developed world was in a deflationary condition, and most didn't realize it. Money was scarce (so were jobs), investment in industry ground to a halt as those with money were hoarding it, and the whole economy pretty much stopped. If money is the fuel of progress, the economy ran out of fuel and stopped running. That is deflation taken to an extreme.

So why does the Fed want a little bit of ongoing inflation? Some theories suggest that inflation has an inverse relationship with unemployment. According to a theory that prevailed for years, in order to drop unemployment (and therefore put more people to work), an economy needs to have a little bit of inflation. This is known as the *Phillips curve* and was one of the toughest concepts for the authors when we encountered this in college. Try as we might, we just couldn't conceive of how the two were directly inversely related. Of course, now we know why we had so much trouble with the concept: the curve has largely been debunked nowadays and shown to be wrong! However, it probably won't surprise you to know that many in government and economics still believe in it, and undergrads somewhere are perhaps still tortured by it as we were.

The other reason the Fed wants a little inflation is because they are convinced that it helps the economy expand. They know that the extra money flowing into the economy ends up in the markets, which goes to the corporations, which gives them more capital to invest, which allows them to expand. Whether or not things work this tidily in the real world is also up for debate.

Finally, the Fed (among other central bankers around the world) is terrified of deflation for the reasons listed above. Therefore, they will take a little bit of the "devil they know" rather than the devil they don't want to meet, erring on the side of inflation as long as it keeps them away from deflation.

Deflation, then, makes your money's purchasing power stronger, while inflation makes it weaker. If your investments are returning, let's say, 4 percent a year, but inflation is running at 3 percent, then you are only really growing your wealth by 1 percent, what investors call the "real rate of return." Since you will likely be fighting the headwind of inflation the most, it should never be ignored when looking at the investment returns on your assets.

So there you have it. The world financial system is tweaked and tampered with by unelected central bankers who move interest rates and money supplies around in an attempt to control outcomes. Their work is very controversial and not entirely proven, and it will have enormous consequences for your assets. This is why it is important to have at least a cursory understanding of it all. Just as with all the risk factors we are discussing, there are investing strategies to "hedge" against the effects of inflation and deflation, which we'll cover later.

Politics

This one is probably obvious, but the political environment can have a big impact on your assets. Certified Financial Planner Paul Mladjenovic said it this way: "If companies were fish, politics and government policies (such as taxes, laws, and regulations) would be the pond. In the same way that fish die in a toxic or polluted pond, politics and government policies can kill companies."

Let's give an extreme example. Let's say you own stock in a lumber company operating out of a country in South America. If the government of that country undergoes a coup d'état and there is a bloody change of leadership, this unrest can directly impact the value of your holdings. What if the government "nationalizes" (meaning confiscates or steals) the company you own stock in? Most likely, in such a scenario the value of your stock goes to zero.

In a presidential election year there is often market unrest in the United States. Wars between countries can affect oil prices, which directly impact stock valuations around the globe. We live in an increasingly interconnected world, and something that happens in one place affects values in another. The unrest, fear, and volatility that result from shocks around the world can circle back around and affect your portfolio.

Economics/Market Forces/Supply and Demand

In the normal course of events, economic forces also circle the globe and have their way with asset valuations. An oil glut will drive down oil prices and thereby impact a whole assortment of related industries. A drought can make grain scarce and therefore costly, affecting the margins of grocers and the price of wheat on the commodity exchanges. The possibilities are endless and occur all the time. Scarcity and abundance drive prices up and down, respectively. All of this can have at least an indirect effect on the value of your assets.

Regulations

Governments and the laws they enact can obviously have a direct bearing on your finances. For instance, for a period of decades, United States citizens were prohibited from owning gold! Imagine having a stash of gold bullion in your investment portfolio when your government up and declares it illegal. This is an extreme example, but these types of things can and do happen.

More likely are the regulations that affect industries or sectors in which you've invested. What if environmental regulations are passed that make it harder for the mining companies you've invested in to do their jobs? While this may be good for the environment, it might not be good at that moment for your holdings. Or what if you own stock in a solar company that a government decides to subsidize (give free money to)? In one of these cases your investment would probably take a hit; in the other it would likely soar. These are typical of the types of things that can happen to your assets (although, of course, the positive kind don't seem to happen nearly as often as the negative kind).

Much of what there is to invest in is based upon business. Businesses are what make the economy go around (despite the politicians, economists, and central bankers who think *they* make the economy run). Unfortunately, the trend seems to be for more and more regulations to be attached to businesses. The burden of regulation on the engine of business seems to grow over time like a burgeoning coral reef. Just look at the following list of regulations affecting most businesses in the United States, as assembled by financial commentator Peter Schiff.

- Social Security payment on behalf of all employees
- Unemployment insurance from 2 to 6 percent
- Worker's compensation payments up to 5 percent in some states
- Local employment taxes (1 to 2 percent)
- Legal liability
- Affordable Health Care Act payments on behalf of each employee
- Americans with Disabilities Act
- Environmental regulations
- Licensing laws
- Minimum wage laws
- Consumer protection laws
- Unionization rules

- Anti-discriminatory laws
- Safety rules
- Local building codes
- Rules governing employee benefit programs

While some or even many of these regulations have intended outcomes we would all agree are desirable, they certainly stack up a lot of drag on a business's ability to operate. This in turn affects the profitability of anyone who invests in or owns such businesses.

Taxes

Didn't we already talk about these? See, we told you there was no escaping them. Here they are creeping into yet another chapter. But that's how taxes are—pervasive. They end up everywhere. And as we said before, taxes will likely be the largest headwind you'll face when building up your collection of assets.

You will be taxed on the money you earn as income. And then you will be taxed on the gains made by your investments of that income. You will also be taxed on the dividends and income you make from your assets. Ready for another list? Here is a quick one demonstrating just how much taxation is out there for the would-be accumulator of assets.

- Federal income tax
- State income tax
- Local income tax
- Social Security
- Medicare Part D
- Affordable Health Care tax
- Property tax
- Capital gains tax

- Gasoline tax
- Sales tax
- Inheritance tax
- Telephone use tax
- Hotel stay tax
- Utility taxes
- Vehicle registrations
- Licenses

When accumulating assets that generate cash flow, it is very unwise to ignore the tax implications along the way. Be sure to find a competent accountant/tax planner to help advise you through the years as you grow in financial stature. The more you make and the more you invest, the more this will matter.

Advice

Believe it or not, one of the most expensive things you will ever encounter is advice. The Securities Industry Association conducted a survey of investors in 2002 and found that 17 percent of them depended most heavily for investment advice on a spouse or friend, 2 percent on a banker, 16 percent on a broker, 10 percent on financial publications, 24 percent on a financial planner, 8 percent on the Internet, and 3 percent on financial television. So it seems people aren't quite sure where to get sound financial advice, so they seek it anywhere and everywhere. No matter how many times it has been proven to be catastrophic, the belief in the "hot stock tip from the shoeshine boy" just doesn't go away.

Our first warning is to be careful whom you listen to; they may be broke! But our second warning is to be careful whom you listen to; they may be in a position to make money off of you! Beware advisers who profit when you act upon their advice.

We must admit right up front that we are a little tainted. We've both had experiences with "experts" who "advised" us to handle our money in ways that ended up costing us millions of dollars. We were given bad advice about how to structure some corporations for our different cash flows. We have had negligent "money managers" overtrade our accounts, racking up nice fees for themselves (and tax liabilities for us) but no appreciable gains in the accounts. In one case, an IRA that was being cared for by a "professional" lost half its value over the course of ten years during one of the strongest bull markets in history! Is that the professional's fault? No, not really. It was *our* money. Ultimately, how it was being cared for was *our* responsibility. There is no excuse for these kinds of results if the owner of the assets is watching them properly, which we weren't.

Lesson learned: nobody will care as much about your money as you. Ever. So no matter how much you make, how busy you get, or how much you trust an adviser, never (we repeat, *never!*) totally hand over the reins of your assets to somebody else. *Always* keep an eye on your own affairs. Benjamin Graham wrote, "Do not let anyone else run your business, unless (1) you can supervise his performance with adequate care and comprehension or (2) you have unusually strong reasons for placing implicit confidence in his integrity and ability."

Here is the challenge: money is complicated. There is a lot to know (that's one of the reasons for this book). If you are going to become an expert at your trade, which is what brings in the cash in the first place, then you don't really have the time or mental bandwidth to *also* become an expert in what to do *with* your money. You must rely on others to give you competent advice. But competence is hard to find. That is why it's a good idea to at least learn the basics we will give you in this book, so, as the sailors say, you can keep a "weather eye" on your advisers and what they are doing with your money.

Now don't get us wrong. There are plenty of honest investment advisers and money managers out there. Just the fact that someone makes a commission by selling you something doesn't make them crooked (after all, we sold you this book, and you can ask our moms, we're as pure as the driven snow)! Still, there is a growing alternative right now in the financial world that we particularly like called a *fee-based fiduciary*. This is a trained professional adviser who recommends investment strategies but doesn't make any commissions on those strategies. Instead, you pay them a flat fee, or perhaps an hourly rate, for their advice.

What makes this arrangement so nice is that they can give you totally unbiased direction on what is best for your situation. You don't have to worry about whether they have a slight conflict of interest or hidden motive behind what they are telling you. Additionally, since their income is not tied to any particular investment product, company, or even category, they are free to give you broader advice, potentially covering everything from life insurance to annuities to stocks and bonds and even real estate and commodities. We would highly recommend at least interviewing several of these types of advisers until you find one who seems extremely competent and whom you feel you can trust. Their advice will be worth their fees. But again, no matter whom you find and how much you trust them, always stay involved in your own financial affairs, always keep an eye on everything that is going on, and apply the lessons you will pick up from this book (which are taken not from us, but from the most successful investors of all time) to make sure things stay on track.

Liquidity

Liquidity is a term that describes how easily you can access your money once you've put it into a particular investment. For example, a savings account is very liquid, as all you need to do to get your money back is make a withdrawal. A commercial rental property, on the other hand, is very *illiquid*, meaning it could take months or even years to get your money back out of it. (Don't even talk to us about restaurants!) Some hedge funds can take several years to free up your money, while angel and venture investing may take even longer (that is, if you don't lose your money entirely; did we mention restaurants?).

Liquidity is important because you never know what will happen in life and when you will need access to some funds, or how much. For this reason, many advisers will tell you to diversify your liquidity, meaning maintain a range of ease of redemption across your various investments. Have a decent amount of money you can get your hands on right away in case you need to (remember the emergency fund?), have other money you can get within a few days, and have still more that you can get within a matter of weeks. Finally, if you have a portion of your portfolio invested in long-term illiquid vehicles like those described above, beware that it may take a long time for you to get access to it.

Liquidity is a risk factor because sometimes markets move quickly. Also, it's a fact that they tend to move most quickly when moving downward. Picture the old photographs from the Great Depression when people were stacked up outside the doors of banks trying to "liquidate" their savings accounts. We rarely hear the stories of "rich" people who have all their money tied up in real estate, and on paper, at least, are worth millions, but when a financial calamity comes along, they can't get their hands on enough cash to keep the proverbial wolf away from the door. It happens. This is one reason we think it's a good idea to at least consider spreading your investments over a wide range of liquidity (or at least erring on the liquid side, depending upon your tolerance for risk).

In plain English: Always keep enough money readily at hand for minor and even major calamities. Never tie up too large a portion of your funds in something you can't get them back out of if necessary.

Theft, Fraud, and Default

The Bible says, "Do not store up for yourselves treasures on earth, where moth and rust destroy, and where thieves break in and steal. But store up for yourselves treasures in heaven, where neither moth nor rust destroys, and where thieves do not break in and steal; for where your treasure is, there your heart will be also." Entire books have been written on this passage, and it goes beyond our purpose here to expound upon it in full (though we would be delighted if you contemplated its meanings and made sure to keep money from taking the central role in your life), but one thing to notice immediately is that thievery was going on way back over two thousand years ago! (Not to mention those doggone moths.)

Like it or not, when you prosper financially, you become a target. Protecting against the possibility of theft is one reason we encouraged you back in chapter 3 to make sure you are properly insured. But there are other types of "theft" to guard against beyond just the cat burglar type. Hucksters in shiny suits will come along and try to fox you out of your wealth. (Sometimes they are the slippery lack-of-integrity types, but other times they're the well-meaning but ignorant-as-a-sack-of-hammers type. Both are equally dangerous.) You will be approached by all sorts of people offering all kinds of opportunities or services that mostly just end up taking your money. Everyone has an investment idea that is *sure* to succeed with the proper funding. Allow us to relate something out of our own personal experience: if someone needs your money that badly, they don't qualify for it. Consider yourself warned: the more money you make, the more you'll have to dig in your heels to keep people from filching it from you. You must learn to say no a lot—or else be prepared to lose a lot of your money.

If you don't exercise due diligence and deeply investigate any-where and everywhere you put your money (and sometimes even if you do), there will be times when the investment totally evaporates. This is called default, and it means that your money is gone forever. From the number of times we've had this happen, we can tell you one good strategy for investing: *when in doubt, don't!* Don't get sucked into swinging for the bleachers by someone who doesn't even know how to hit the ball. You will just strike out.

> **Don't get sucked into swinging for the bleachers by someone who doesn't even know how to hit the ball.**

There is an entire world of ven-ture capital and angel investing in which diligent professionals work hard to investigate opportuni-ties before investing in them, and more often than not, they *still* get it wrong. Like so many investments, unless you can dedicate the time to become a qualified expert yourself in that category, you are probably much better to stay away entirely. At least mini-mize your investment in such speculations so that if you lost it all, you would barely care.

Yourself

The final risk factor we'll consider here is perhaps the biggest one of all—*you!* Jason Zweig wrote, "Ultimately, financial risk re-sides not in what kinds of investments you have, but in what kind of investor you are. If you want to know what risk really is, go to the nearest bathroom and step up to the mirror. *That's* risk, gaz-ing back at you from the glass."

Wait a minute, you might be thinking. *You just told us that we shouldn't just hand over our investments to someone else—that we ourselves had to stay in charge of our own money. Why would we do that if we are our own biggest risk factor?* Good question. The reason is simple: if you are the owner of your money, you are ultimately responsible for its care and feeding. As we said before, no one will be as concerned about your money as you, no matter what, ever. Therefore, your best chance is to get educated on finances yourself, at least to some degree. And then learn the habits of the wealthy so you can emulate them, all the while keeping yourself from messing things up through lapses in judgment or emotional responses.

> "Ultimately, financial risk resides not in what kinds of investments you have, but in what kind of investor you are."
> —Jason Zweig

An old story is told of a young preacher getting his first chance to preach. He prepares his sermon for weeks and practices in front of the mirror. Finally the big day comes. When it is his turn to ascend the rostrum, he does so with gusto. Full of pride and power, he strides to the pulpit and proceeds to deliver the most average sermon in the history of the church. As he descends the stairs, he realizes his mediocrity and almost slinks from view. Later, when he asks the senior pastor for advice, the wiser older man simply says, "If you'd gone up the way you came down, you'd have come down the way you went up."

There was nothing wrong, apparently, with the content of the young man's sermon. What made his delivery so average was his prideful attitude. If he'd been a bit more humble and contrite on the way up, he'd have been able to do justice to the message and leave the scene with the satisfaction of a job well done. Unfortunately, he did the opposite.

We like this little story, and we think it applies here. Approach your finances with the respect and humility they deserve. Realize that this is an enormous stewardship you've been given and that, if you've been blessed to receive money and the health and wherewithal to start accumulating a portfolio of assets, such a privilege comes with real responsibility. Approach it with the proper humility and an eagerness to learn. Be watchful and not rash. Have patience, and be diligent, focusing on the long term. Be mature, and resist the urge to get something for nothing, to "strike it rich," or to "hit the big one." With the proper maturity and informed approach to the topic, you'll be insulated against the prideful "animal spirits" that seem to take hold of investors and lead them to ruin. Playing with fire is dangerous, but working with fire is one of life's necessities. Don't play with your finances. You will only get burned.

PART III

ASSET ALLOCATION PLAN

HOW MUCH MONEY YOU WILL KEEP IN DIFFERENT INVESTMENT CATEGORIES

SIX

Assets Explained – Part I The Left Side of the Risk Meter

"Most investors pay way, way too much to middlemen who suck the lifeblood out of portfolios."
—RUSSELL WILD

So far you've determined your overall Comprehensive Financial Plan, which includes how you will earn, save, spend, and invest your money. We talked through the idea that the wealthy use their money to acquire assets, while the middle class use theirs to buy stuff they want. In fact, you can always tell the financial maturity of someone once they come into some money. Do they spend (and overspend) it on *things*? Or do they channel it into *assets*? Anyway, you have now learned that the game is to accumulate assets over time, flowing money from the left side of Robert Kiyosaki's Cashflow Quadrant over to the right side. Your entire Comprehensive Financial Plan is geared toward that over-arching theme.

You've also considered your Investment Policy, which will guide you in acquiring quality assets for the long term, using tactics such as paying yourself first and dollar cost averaging instead of trying to "beat the market." And you learned about a whole list of risk factors that you are up against. Now it's time to start taking a look at the bullets you'll load into your portfolio gun, which is how you'll fight back against those risk factors and prosper over time. Those bullets are the individual assets in which you can invest.

If you'll look inside the dust jacket of the hardcover version of this book, or on page 107, you'll see a diagram we call the *Risk Meter*. The idea is that there is a general range of riskiness from low to high that can be represented by something like a thermometer. We have already discussed the concept of risk and seen that most experts cannot entirely agree on this enormous subject, but for the purposes of this exercise, the relative magnitude of the items on this diagram will suffice. What we want to do is generally familiarize you with the full range of assets available to the individual investor and do so in a way that relates them to each other in terms of risk and sophistication.

If you'll remember the YOU, Inc. Investment Hierarchy, this Risk Meter is just an exploded view of its top three levels (levels 5, 6, and 7). Just as we discussed with the hierarchy, a wise approach would be to begin at the bottom and work upward from safer toward riskier (or simpler toward more sophisticated) assets. The amount and specifics will depend upon your individual situation and risk appetite, which we'll discuss later.

Finally, at the risk (pun unavoidable!) of repeating ourselves, remember that you should really only be investing at the top of the YOU, Inc. Hierarchy once you've exhausted the amount you can invest in yourself and whatever business you may have decided to build. This is because you and your business are directly under your control, while everything we're going to discuss from here onward is, at varying degrees, outside your direct control. The principle is that the best investment

> **The best investment you can ever make is the one over which you retain the most control.**

you can ever make is the one over which you retain the most control. The rest of this stuff is for what's left over after you've done that.

Okay, with that final caveat, let's proceed through the list of assets you may choose to begin acquiring.

Gold (and Silver)

For many people around the world gold is the safest asset of them all. When economies get uncertain, there is usually a general "flight to safety" into gold. Gold enthusiasts, often called "gold bugs," argue that gold itself never really changes in value. Their strong argument points out that around gold fluctuate the world's fiat currencies—paper currencies backed by nothing other than government dictate; hence the French word *fiat*, meaning "to declare," which pretty much describes all the currencies in the world today.

Consider the following chart, which shows the relationship between the US dollar and the dollar price of gold.

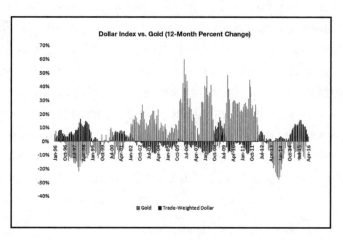

macrotrends.net

As the dollar strengthens, gold weakens. And as the dollar weakens, gold goes up. This is because if dollars weaken, it takes more of them to buy that same ounce of gold. According to QuandryFX on seekingalpha.com, "Now, the Federal Reserve is increasing interest rates, which historically has led to collapses in the dollar every single time. On the basis of the dollar alone, investors should consider purchasing gold."[1]

One ounce of gold back in the days of the Roman Empire would buy one man's toga, tunic, and sandals; during the Colonial era it would buy one suit and related accoutrements for a gentleman about town; and again today (when gold, at the time of this writing, is valued at approximately $1250 US) it will buy a nice men's suit complete with shoes, belt, shirt, and tie. It seems as if the relative purchasing power of element #79 on the periodic table stays pretty constant. This doesn't mean that it doesn't experience price fluctuations in its valuation due to speculation on the open market, but on the whole, gold seems to remain pretty constant against the macro trends working their way through human history.

For this reason, many people feel that gold is the safest investment one can make. If you buy into the view that gold simply retains its value against all comers, then it is best perhaps looked at not as an investment, per se, in which one would expect a *return*, but rather a *store of value*. Market expert James Rickards wrote, "Gold is money, and money has no yield because it has no risk. Money can be a medium of exchange, a store of value, and a unit of account, but true money is *not* a risk asset. To get a return on an investment, you have to take a risk. With gold, where is the risk? There is no maturity risk, because it's just gold. It won't 'ma-

---

1 This recommendation comes at a time when interest rates around the world have been lowered to zero and even, in some cases, below zero. As a result, at the time of the above quote, the Federal Reserve had indicated that it intended to consistently raise rates over the next few years.

ture' into gold five years from now; it is gold today, and always will be. Gold has no issuer risk, because nobody issues it. If you own it, you own it. It's not anyone else's liability. There's no commodity risk. With commodities there are other risks to consider. When you buy corn, you have to worry: Does it have bugs in it? Is it good corn or bad corn? It's the same with oil; there are seventy-five grades of oil around the world. But pure gold is an element . . . [it's] always just gold" (emphasis his).

By putting your money into gold, you are putting it beyond the reach of central banks and governments. You are, in effect, "parking" the fruits of your labor into something that is *tamper-proof*. Think of it as "freezing your fruit." If you put some summer strawberries into plastic bags and in the freezer to be enjoyed in the off-season, you wouldn't be disappointed to pull your berries out of the freezer and discover that they hadn't multiplied. You'd be happy just to have your fruit in the winter, perfectly preserved. In the view of many, this is the function of gold. You don't put your money into it in order to "grow" it in value, to receive dividends, or a yield. You do so simply to keep or freeze its value.

As author George R. R. Martin wrote in his world-famous book *Game of Thrones*, "Winter is coming." Financially speaking, there is always another winter coming. Freezing some of your fruit in preparation for the next winter makes plain good sense.

Much of the investing world has recently come around to share this view (at least to some degree). For instance, Ray Dalio, manager of the largest hedge fund in the world, recommends that individual investors keep 7.5 percent of their personal portfolio in gold. Perhaps part of the reason for the growing popularity of gold as an asset class is the ease with which it can be invested in today compared to just a decade or so ago (more on this later when we talk about exchange-traded funds). Perhaps another reason is gold's "performance" over the past twelve years or so, when it has experienced the largest growth in valuation of any asset class. (Again, there is a strong case to be made that this is merely a reflection of the amount the world's fiat money supplies have been inflated, paired with speculation in gold as a safe haven.)

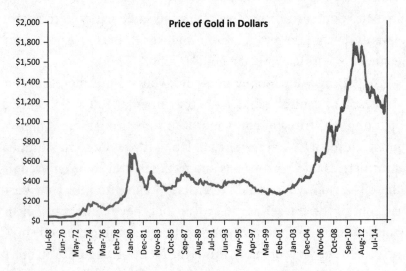

Price of Gold in Dollars

macrotrends.net

At any rate, an individual investor who began dollar cost averaging purchases of gold back in, say, 2003 (as did our friend of whom we spoke earlier), continuing that practice until today, would be very happy to have done so! Her efforts would have outrun almost all the other asset classes we'll describe in this chapter and the next. This is shocking performance, really, when you consider that we are listing gold as the first investment on the Risk Meter because it is one of the *safest*. It's just more proof of Warren Buffett's argument that often the best returns can come from the safest investments.

RISK METER

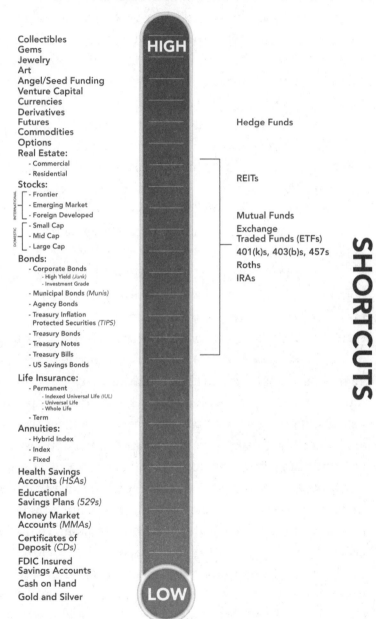

ASSETS

Collectibles
Gems
Jewelry
Art
Angel/Seed Funding
Venture Capital
Currencies
Derivatives
Futures
Commodities
Options
Real Estate:
- Commercial
- Residential
Stocks:
INTERNATIONAL
- Frontier
- Emerging Market
- Foreign Developed
DOMESTIC
- Small Cap
- Mid Cap
- Large Cap
Bonds:
- Corporate Bonds
    - High Yield (Junk)
    - Investment Grade
- Municipal Bonds (Munis)
- Agency Bonds
- Treasury Inflation
  Protected Securities (TIPS)
- Treasury Bonds
- Treasury Notes
- Treasury Bills
- US Savings Bonds
Life Insurance:
- Permanent
    - Indexed Universal Life (IUL)
    - Universal Life
    - Whole Life
- Term
Annuities:
- Hybrid Index
- Index
- Fixed
Health Savings
Accounts (HSAs)
Educational
Savings Plans (529s)
Money Market
Accounts (MMAs)
Certificates of
Deposit (CDs)
FDIC Insured
Savings Accounts
Cash on Hand
Gold and Silver

HIGH

LOW

SHORTCUTS

Hedge Funds

REITs

Mutual Funds
Exchange
Traded Funds (ETFs)
401(k)s, 403(b)s, 457s
Roths
IRAs

*The risk level of each of these assets relative to each other is very general and open for much
debate. This is intended to serve only as a very loose guide.

So what about silver? Silver has almost always been a kind of little brother to gold. It, too, has some value as a precious metal, but more than that, it is used in industrial applications. For instance, silver is a component in most solar panels and in a lot of circuit board assembly. Silver is good to own along with gold as a safety investment, US coins prior to the year 1965 being one preferred option (because of their recognizability in case of a true societal calamity). One can envision being able to buy scarce food and resources with such a well-known, authentic piece of silver. But silver is also not worth very much with respect to its weight and therefore is not as efficient a store of wealth as is gold. Any significant dollar amount of silver would weigh more than a person could carry. Also, it is in much greater supply, is mined much more easily and widely, and therefore will likely never be as rare or as fit for "storing value" as will gold.

Many experts simply recommend supplementing your gold holdings with "spendable" silver (such as the US coins just mentioned) or easily verified silver rounds and smaller bars. However, one other thing to consider is that if silver really has a type of "peg" to the price of gold, meaning a multiplier that ties it to gold, then if gold hits the highs many are saying it must, silver too would race upward. Since it costs less in dollars per ounce, its percentage return would be much, much higher than would gold's. For this reason some people are more enthusiastic about accumulating silver than about gold. And, of course, since it is much cheaper than gold per ounce, it is more accessible to the individual investor of more modest means. In summary, it is probably a good idea to accumulate both, making your own decisions about the quantity of each based upon the above factors.

There is one big drawback to accumulating silver and gold, at least in the United States. For some crazy reason, the US tax code considers gold and silver to be "collectibles" and therefore subject to a special 28 percent capital gains tax. This is doubly unfair when you realize that one of the biggest reasons for the increase in the dollar price of these metals is the depreciation of the dollar itself, which is caused by the government (at least, by the Federal Reserve, which is granted its very existence by the federal government)! So they devalue the purchasing power of the dollar on one hand, which drives up the dollar price of gold and silver, and then with the other hand they collect 28 percent from us on the resulting price change. You can't make this stuff up.

So far we've been discussing the accumulation of gold and silver in physical form, often called bullion (in addition to the coins mentioned above). But the silver and gold markets can also be accessed in a few other ways. For instance, one could buy gold mining stocks, which are much more volatile than the spot price of gold, but should still do quite well if the gold market zooms upward. Also, certain exchange-traded funds (ETFs), which we'll cover in detail later in this chapter, track the spot prices of gold and silver. By buying these "paper" vehicles, which can be bought and sold like a stock, one can benefit from the price movement of precious metals without actually having to take physical possession of the metals themselves. This is good for price investing but does nothing for calamity protection. Just something to consider.

Cash on Hand

There is nothing like cold, hard cash. In a world of electronic banking, credit cards, and the threat that governments will stop allowing cash at all (or at least get rid of large bills), having a stock of actual cash has some appeal to a lot of people. The old instinct of stuffing a mattress is alive and well. Again, part of the lure of this approach is having some money that is tamperproof and out of anyone else's grubby hands. It is also immediately available and as liquid as possible when it is in your own possession. You will never be part of a bank run if you are your own bank. There are some extreme examples of this. We know of a relative who won't even use banks because of his credit issues in the past and bank accounts being swept by government agencies. Like a terrorist off the grid, this person uses only cash for everything.

While such extremes are not recommended, it might be a good idea to have a little cash reserve tucked safely away someplace. The downside, of course, is that inflation eats away at the spending power of cash that is sitting outside of any kind of interest-bearing account. Also, keeping lots of cash around may present a safety risk for your family. Therefore, most advisers recommend having some cash on hand (the amount will differ based upon your particular circumstances), storing it prudently in a safe deposit box at a bank or a private vault company. Again, there are limitations and slight risks with each of these answers, but having some easily accessed cash is probably a good idea.

FDIC Insured Savings

Speaking of bank runs, they led to some interesting government programs in the United States (and many other countries now have similar setups). One was the creation of something called the Federal Deposit Insurance Corporation. The idea is that your savings in a bank are protected by the "full faith and credit of the US Government" (a phrase borrowed from the clause of the same name in the US Constitution) up to a deposit amount of $250,000 (at the time of this writing). This means that if a bank should fail and close its doors, taking your deposited money down with it, the US Government itself will pay you back the lost amount. While this sounds pretty reassuring, it may be helpful to remember our discussion about inflation from the previous chapter, understanding that in many cases if banks are failing and it is necessary for the government to bail out the bank's customers, there's a good chance the currency itself is in trouble.

Additionally, the government will just create the new money out of thin air, causing more inflation (assuming the issue isn't at just one isolated bank), meaning that the money they are giving really isn't worth all that much anyway. At least, that's the opinion of the skeptics of the FDIC program. But still, it's better than a sharp stick in the eye! And you may as well deposit your funds in accounts that have that protection rather than those that do not.

Finally, be aware of a new arrival on the banking scene: Internet banks. These have no physical branches, only exist online, and (because of a lower resulting cost structure) can offer slightly higher rates of interest on your savings. Many of these are also covered by FDIC. Check them out for yourself, and see if they make sense for you as a way to squeeze out every last drop of possible interest on your savings.

Certificates of Deposit (CDs)

Back when interest rates were higher, a popular savings vehicle was developed called a *certificate of deposit* (or *CD* for short). These basically pay a higher interest rate than regular savings in exchange for you, the depositor, agreeing to forgo access to your money for some predetermined amount of time (six months, one year, two years, etc.). If you need to withdraw your money sooner than the time frame specified, you will have to pay a penalty. In a way, such restricted access to your funds can be a good thing. Remember from the last chapter that one of the biggest risk factors to your investments is *you* (or at least your spouse)! For many people, keeping their funds out of their own reach is a helpful deterrent to wasteful spending.

Many certificates of deposit are also FDIC insured. Their popularity has waned in recent years due to ridiculously low interest rates that don't even outrun inflation. Still, CDs may make sense for some people in certain situations or for small portions of your money that you don't want to invest elsewhere. And it is always possible that higher interest rates will one day return. One other slight drawback when investing in CDs is that you can't add to them with dollar cost averaging. Instead, if you want to make ongoing investments into this type of vehicle, it will require obtaining a new certificate of deposit each time, which is impractical.

Money Market Accounts (MMAs)

Money market accounts pay higher rates of interest than regular savings accounts, and sometimes more than CDs, but instead of promising your money for a specific amount of time, you usually have to meet a minimum deposit requirement. The FDIC also insures many money market accounts.

Here is a table to help sort out the three bank deposit types:

ACCOUNT TYPE	INTEREST PAID	TIME PERIOD REQUIRED?	MINIMUM BALANCE REQUIRED?
SAVINGS ACCOUNT	LOW	NO	NOT USUALLY
CD	HIGHER	YES	NO
MONEY MARKET	HIGHER	NO	YES

Again, each of these three vehicles, while easy to understand and access (simply visit your local bank branch or check out an Internet bank), are not much more than convenient ways to earn a little gain on your money. They should not be considered very good investments (at least at current interest rate levels in the world) because they don't even keep up with inflation. Most investors will use them for specific purposes for a short time, perhaps when moving money between more lucrative investments, for instance. In fact, most brokerage accounts (which we'll discuss in more detail later) that allow you to invest your money in a variety of vehicles offer money market accounts for when your money is not being used for those investments.

Health Savings Accounts (HSAs) and
Educational Savings Plans (529s)

In the United States there are a few custom tax-advantaged savings accounts that were created to give the taxpayer a break when saving for a specific purpose. One is called a *health savings account* (HSA). An HSA allows people below a certain income limit, who also have high-deductible medical plans, to save money toward their medical expenses. The idea is that the money can be put into the savings account on a pretax basis, and then the contributions made to the account remain there from year to year until used. The interest and other earnings in the account grow tax free. There are annual contribution limits, of course, and rules about what constitutes an allowable withdrawal expense. Withdrawals not used for the approved uses are subject to income tax and a 20 percent penalty.

There is also a type of plan designed to offer tax-advantaged saving toward college expenses. These vary a bit from state to state, but earnings in *529 plans* are not subject to federal taxation and in many cases not subject to state taxes either. These tax advantages only apply, however, as long as the withdrawals from a 529 account are used for eligible educational expenses such as tuition, room and board, etc.

Both HSAs and 529s are offered by brokerage firms and banks and usually allow the investor access to a fairly broad range of investment vehicles. Overall, tax-advantaged accounts of any kind are a good idea, and you should be sure to check your specific situation to see if they make sense for you.

Annuities

Remember that as we ascend the list on the left side of the Risk Meter, we are considering more and more sophisticated investment vehicles. This next one, *annuities*, ushers us into a higher level of complexity, but also should bring more pleasing returns.

Annuities are ancient investment vehicles that appear to have begun with the Romans. Back then, a Roman citizen would make a one-time payment and then receive annual payments back for the rest of his lifetime. The idea was that most people would die before collecting all their money back through the annual payments, leaving enough funds to pay the survivors in perpetuity. The result was a *guaranteed lifetime income*. Ultimately, that's the attractiveness of an annuity today (without having to hope that everybody else dies off). Annuities (structured properly, meaning the kind that has a "guaranteed income rider") are pretty much the only investment vehicle that can completely guarantee you will not run out of money at the end of your life.

> **Annuities are pretty much the only investment vehicle that can completely guarantee you will not run out of money at the end of your life.**

There are several different types of annuities (you knew we were going to say that!), but three of the biggest categories are:

1. Fixed
2. Indexed
3. Hybrid indexed

A *fixed annuity* takes your lump sum payment and promises you a specific amount of money back each year based upon how much you originally put in and how long you wait to begin receiving the payments. The older you are before you turn on the payments, the higher the annual money you'll receive. If you have the guaranteed income rider attached to one of these, this amount of money will continue until you die.

An *indexed annuity* works much the same way, except the amount of money available from which to start paying you, once you turn payments on, is determined by a "variable" performance over time of a certain index (the same indices to which we've referred earlier). In this way, if the S&P 500 takes off over the course of the rest of your life, the payments of your annuity will be much larger than if it languishes during that period. It's a risk, but it generally offers a pretty nice upside.

A *hybrid indexed annuity* is a combination of the two types just described. The upside of the return is tied to some index, but there is a guaranteed minimum return on the low side.

Like many of the investment vehicles we will cover, annuities have their critics. One criticism is that once you put your money into an annuity, you cannot get it back out without incurring significant penalties. Another is that if the remainder of your annuity is bequeathed to your beneficiaries upon your death, they must pay income taxes on it (which they do *not* have to do when receiving your universal life insurance death benefit payout, by way of comparison). Further, like almost anything else, unscrupulous salespeople have made a bad name for annuities with high commissions and poorly performing products. This has changed quite a bit in recent times, however, and many good, very affordable annuity products don't even come from life insurance companies but can be purchased directly from money management firms such as Vanguard.

Finally, there will always be those who claim that complicated investments must not be good ones, and annuities certainly can seem complicated. Still, a properly chosen annuity is the best guaranteed lifetime income available today and should be given serious consideration for any retirement plan. As we'll cover later, annuities can be purchased in midlife or even upon retirement and don't necessarily have to be part of your portfolio until those later ages. Again, as with everything we're discussing, always seek competent counsel for your specific situation.

Life Insurance

We've already sufficiently covered the primary types of life insurance in chapter 3. However, allow us to present a quick summary here for the sake of a complete Risk Meter. We consider it to be a relatively safe investment vehicle (and therefore right near annuities on the scale) because insurance companies are almost notorious for their financial stability. Think about it: when is the last time you heard about an insurance company going out of business? Besides, in the United States, each individual state forces the life insurance companies who operate within their borders to back each other's policies in case any of the other companies defaults. So even if your particular company goes under, a consortium of others will be forced by law to uphold your policy. That seems pretty safe to us. Still, you should check the rating of the provider you are considering and make sure they are rated at least an "A."

Life insurance can do much more than simply provide a death benefit to your heirs. It can also be a significant and tax-efficient wealth-building vehicle. Also, it can be very valuable in preparing for long-term care should you need extended medical assistance. Don't be too quick to listen to the pat answers critics often give, such as "buy term insurance and invest the rest," or "say no to any type of life insurance that also develops a cash value." For some reason, these two phrases have quite a bit of traction in the marketing that is done to North America's middle class, and unfortunately, it is often heeded. But the wealthy do not agree and don't behave that way. They buy massive cash value life insurance policies and max them out (even large companies do so). As you grow in financial stature, ask yourself if it might be a good idea for you to emulate their example. Then shop around until you can find an agent who will build you a policy that meets your needs and maximizes your wealth building. As always, shop around.

Bonds (also known as Fixed Income Securities)

The worldwide bond market is huge. At approximately $95 trillion, it is fully $40 trillion larger than the total of all the stocks in the world! And the sheer variety of bonds available to invest in is mind-blowing.

A bond is nothing more than a contract to pay back a certain amount of money with interest. Sounds simple enough, right? Well, the fact that bonds are openly traded in public markets complicates things. As this happens, their prices fluctuate. Remember money market accounts? A money market account is an instrument in which your principal is secure, but your interest rate fluctuates every day. A bond is the opposite. The interest rate is fixed, but the price fluctuates every day.

A bond is issued with a particular *face amount*, also called *par value* or *principal*. For some reason, most bonds are issued with a face amount of $1,000. Every bond also pays a rate of interest, called its *coupon rate*. Usually, this coupon rate is fixed over the life of the bond (this is why bonds are called *fixed income* securities). The coupon rate is a percentage of the face amount and is customarily paid out to the bondholder twice a year. Further, a bond is issued for a specific period of time, called its *maturity*.

Get ready for a little complication. The *yield* of a bond is different than its *interest rate/coupon rate*. The yield is the *effective* interest rate after taking into account the market-adjusted price of the bond. The coupon rate is fixed, but the yield changes as the bond's market price changes. So if the price of a bond falls in the market, the yield would go higher than the coupon rate. This is because the yield equals the money being paid out each year divided by the market price of the bond.

Ready for an example? Let's say your county issues $1,000 bonds to raise money to build a park, and the coupon rate of those bonds is 3%. This would equate to $30 per year being paid out by your county to the holder of one of these bonds, or $15 twice a year. These payment amounts are set in stone. Then at maturity (when the time period for the bond is up), your county pays back to the holder of the bond the full $1,000. So far so good. But before the bond gets to its maturity date, it trades from person to person on the bond market. Let's say it eventually trades down from its original $1,000 to a price of $900. It is still paying the $30 per year, however. So 30 divided by 900 equals a 3.33% yield, which is higher than the original 3% coupon rate. And of course the opposite would hold true, too. The yield would go down if the price of the bond went up (because the dollar amount paid out each year remains constant). Don't worry, that's as far as we'll go.

The point with bonds is that historically they have been considered one of the safest investments around, because the dollar amount of the annual payments is guaranteed. The only way the holder of a bond does not get her money is if the issuer of the bond defaults (goes out of business, goes bankrupt, etc.).[2] So the risk of a bond is dependent upon the solvency of its issuer. And since most issuers of bonds are governments and large corporations, the chance of default has historically been pretty low.

The other risk is due to interest rates changing—not the interest rates/coupon rates of the bonds when they are originally issued, which don't change; we mean the interest rates set by the

---

2   There actually is another way we won't go into, which is when a bond is callable.

Federal Reserve, as we described earlier. If those interest rates go up, the price of bonds goes down, because suddenly new bonds paying more money are available, making previous bonds paying a lower amount worth less. Therefore, on the open market, the price of the older bonds must come down until their yields match the coupon rates of the new bonds being issued (which for the most part will correspond to the interest rate being set by the Fed). So the other risk to bondholders is that interest rates will go up and thereby decrease the value of their bonds.

Those are the two risks: outright default and a decrease in value if interest rates rise. However, even with these two possibilities, bonds have usually proven to be much safer and less volatile than stocks and for that reason are very popular investment vehicles. Also important is that market price movement in bonds tends to have very little correlation with stocks, so bonds help in diversifying a portfolio. When the stock market is tanking, bonds usually do their own thing and can even run in the other direction as money pours from stocks into the relative safety of the bond market. We'll talk a lot more about this in chapter 8.

There are many types of bonds. Diversifying your bond exposure will be important, so you'll need to know about these different categories. We'll discuss some of them briefly, just to give you an idea of what's available, beginning with those generally felt to be the least risky. Again, by "riskiness" we are referring to their likelihood of experiencing an outright default on one hand, or wild price swings on the other.

US Savings Bonds

By far the wimpiest (paying the lowest amount of interest) kind of bonds available are US Savings Bonds. They are unique in that they are available in very small dollar amounts (any amount, determined by the purchaser, over $25 but under $1,000), can be bought only directly from the US Treasury, and cannot be marketed in any way. When you buy a US Savings Bond, you must put someone's name and corresponding Social Security number on it, and it thereafter belongs only to them. US Savings Bonds were once very popular as gifts, but now that the fancy paper certificate has been done away with and they are digital just like everything else, this attraction has faded. The paltry amount of interest paid by US Savings Bonds, which is received only once they are redeemed, doesn't usually even keep up with the rate of inflation. For this reason, they are a pretty unappealing investment at this time.

Treasury Bills, Notes, and Bonds

The next categories of bonds are all issued by the US Treasury and are marketable securities. This means that unlike US Savings Bonds, they are not assigned to a particular person and are traded on the open market. They can be purchased directly from the US Treasury, in mutual funds/exchange-traded funds/hedge funds, or through a broker. These instruments are not limited to US citizens; they can be purchased by anyone around the world. The Chinese government, for instance, is an enormous holder of US debt. Almost all of the US Treasury debt (which will hit approximately $20 trillion by the end of 2016) is made up of US Treasury bills, notes, and bonds. The biggest difference between the three is their maturations.

- Treasury bills have a maturity of one year or less
- Treasury notes are between two and ten years
- Treasury bonds range from ten to thirty years

The bills are slightly different than the notes and bonds in one other way. Bills have a face value of $100 but sell at a discount from that amount. At the end of the year you redeem them for the full $100. Your gain becomes the difference between what you paid and the $100.

US Treasury notes and bonds work as we described when we introduced bonds in general. They carry a face value of $1,000 and a fixed dollar amount that is paid out twice a year. Their yield changes as their price fluctuates on the open market.

Generally speaking, the longer the maturation period of a bond, the higher the interest it pays. This means that the longer you are willing to tie up your money, the more you will be paid for doing so. But with all these securities being openly traded, you really aren't locked in to holding them until maturity. At any point you can sell them on the market, very similarly to how you would with a stock.

A further consideration is taxes. The interest from US Treasuries is not subject to income tax at the state or local levels.

Finally, as regards liquidity, which you'll remember is the ease with which you can sell an asset you own, US Treasuries are some of the most liquid investments in the world. Since the market is so huge, there is always a willing buyer at market price for a US Treasury security. So you can be pretty confident of being able to get your money out in a pinch if necessary.

The biggest thing to understand about US Treasuries is that they provide one of the safest investment havens in times of economic turmoil. In almost any portfolio allocation, which we'll cover in chapter 8, the experts recommend a large portion of US bonds. This is because they behave differently than stocks and other more volatile investments, and can dampen wild swings in the value of your overall portfolio. Further, the prevailing notion is that the US government, as one of the largest and strongest in the world, is very unlikely to default on its bonds (as Russia did in 1998). US Treasuries are also a place where money flees when the economy spooks investors, and when this happens, the value of your bond holdings goes up (because the prices of the bonds you are holding are driven up by all the new investors in the bond market). Finally, there is something pretty satisfying about knowing that the bonds you hold promise to pay a certain amount of dollars each year you hold them. Many people like the sense of security this brings.

Treasury Inflation-Protected Securities (TIPS)

With fixed income securities, one of the biggest concerns is outrunning inflation. Sure, it's nice to hold a bond that promises to pay you a guaranteed dollar amount twice a year, but what if inflation is higher than the yield you are receiving from the bond and effectively you end up going backward? For instance, your bond in the example above giving you a yield of 3.33 percent would be nice, but not if inflation is running at 4 percent per year. In that scenario you'd actually be *losing* 0.67 percent per year.

To compensate for this situation, the US government came out with something called a Treasury Inflation-Protected Security (commonly called a TIPS), which makes an adjustment to its principal twice a year to account for the inflation rate. So if inflation is 4 percent, adjustments are made to the principal amount on the bond twice that year so that the coupon rate would still apply beyond the inflation rate. So let's say you held a TIPS with a 1 percent coupon rate during a 4 percent inflation rate year, your TIPS would effectively pay at a nominal 5 percent, or 1 percent after inflation.

While this is pretty nice, there are a couple of drawbacks (you knew there would be). First, the coupon rates on TIPS tend to be very low. Second, their prices fluctuate quite a bit. This is because their market is pretty small compared to the huge Treasury market in the other types of bonds, so the price is driven largely by investor sentiment.

Agency Bonds

In addition to the US Treasury, many other US agencies also issue bonds. They include a whole list of acronym organizations such as the Government National Mortgage Association (GNMA), the Private Export Funding Corporation (PEFCO), and the Financial Assistance Corporation (FAC). There are many more! While these are not backed by the "full faith and credit of the US Government" as are US Treasuries, there is an implied guarantee that the United States government will stand behind them.

Most experts agree, however, that these aren't quite as safe as US Treasuries. This is because most of these federal agencies are not really part of the US government but instead are actually something called *government-sponsored enterprises* (or GSEs). These are not necessarily without their troubles, as two of the biggest, Freddie Mac and Fannie Mae—Federal Home Loan Mortgage Corporation [FHLMC] and Federal National Mortgage Association [FNMA]—went into receivership after the housing bubble popped in 2008.

The US government did sweep in and "nationalize" these agencies, keeping them from otherwise going under, so there you go. Still, there is no real guarantee that all agency and GSE bonds will get this kind of support. For this reason, you can consider investments in them to be a little bit higher on the Risk Meter than good old true-blue US Treasuries. But you will generally receive higher coupon rates for taking that slightly higher risk.

Municipal Bonds (Munis)

The US government isn't the only government issuing bonds. Local and state governments of all shapes and sizes are in on the game too. These are called *municipal bonds* (or *munis*). These bonds are issued for any number of reasons, from infrastructure projects (like building parks, as in our example above) to meeting day-to-day operating expenses. Unlike most bonds, munis tend to be issued in denominations of $5,000 (instead of the $1,000 for US Treasuries). They can be purchased directly from their issuer and also through funds or brokers.

There are two main advantages to owning munis. The first is tax considerations. In the United States, municipal bond interest is federal income tax–free. Depending upon the issuer, some munis are exempt from both federal and state income tax (these are called double-tax-free bonds). Some munis, if issued locally to the bondholder, may even be exempt from federal, state, *and* local income tax (called triple-tax-free bonds).

If that weren't enough, municipal bonds sell mostly to individual investors, which means the makeup of their market is quite different from those of other bonds (especially US Treasuries, which are purchased in huge amounts by the biggest governments and institutional investors around the world). This is important because it means that the pricing fluctuations for municipal bonds behave very independently from the rest of the bond market and therefore do a nice job of helping to diversify a portfolio.

One problem with holding municipal bonds is that they are often *callable*. This means that the issuer can call off the agreement and give you back your money before the maturity date. This might not seem like a bad thing, but it usually means that the price of the bond on the market has dropped considerably, and the issuer is taking advantage of that fact to pay off their debt on the cheap. In such a scenario, you may or may not get all your money back.

The relative safety of municipal bonds depends upon the solvency of the issuer. In recent times, city governments (and even some states) have gotten into serious financial trouble. The possibility of an issuer defaulting on a municipal bond is far higher than it is for a US Treasury. For this reason it is important to check the ratings of a muni before buying. (A rating is a grade assigned by experts to a particular bond that should indicate the relative safety of the investment. There are ratings agencies that specialize in providing these across the whole bond market. Moody's, Standard & Poor's, and Fitch are three of the best known.)

The higher you rise in the federal income tax brackets, the more you will want to consider having municipal bonds in your portfolio. However, they don't make much sense to own inside of a tax-advantaged account such as a 401(k) or IRA (Individual Retirement Account). Both of these will be discussed later. Finally, most experts will recommend holding at least some munis for the sake of diversification. We'll get to easy ways to do so in chapter 7.

Corporate Bonds

It probably won't surprise you to learn that governments don't get to have all the fun in the bond market. Corporations also issue bonds. Companies need money to invest and grow, and they can get it in two primary ways: selling little shares of the business to stockholders, and borrowing money by selling bonds.

Corporate bonds tend to outperform Treasuries (meaning their price goes up more) when the economy is good, but they tend to underperform them when the economy does poorly. Corporate bonds have a pretty high correlation of their price movement to the stock market, so they aren't all that great for diversifying your portfolio. Also, if a company goes under, the bondholder could lose all or some of her money. As far as liquidity, corporate bonds are not as liquid as US Treasuries (meaning there are not nearly as many ready buyers for them). And finally, most corporate bonds are callable, as we explained in the municipal bond section.

Just why would anyone want to invest in corporate bonds then? Because they often pay more interest than government bonds. The difference between the two is referred to as "the spread." When the spread gets large enough, investors jump into corporate bonds. The spread usually gets larger when the economy isn't so good. This means that investors are feeling skittish, and corporations need to issue bonds with higher and higher interest rates in order to entice people to buy them.

As with all non-Treasury bonds, the ratings provided by the ratings agencies will be an important guide to help you understand the relative strength of the company issuing the bond. The term *investment grade* refers to corporate bonds that have been given a rating of at least *Baa* by Moody's, or the equivalent *BBB* by Standard & Poor's, or the equivalent *BBB* by Fitch. Any corporate bond below these ratings is called by the name *high yield* or the more famous *junk bond*.

So corporate bonds are broken down into two main categories:

- Investment grade (those that have high ratings)
- High yield, or junk (those with low ratings)

There are also corporate bonds of differing maturations, of course, from short term to intermediate to long term. As with Treasuries, the interest rates are generally higher the longer the maturation.

One final type to at least know about is the *convertible bond*. These are corporately issued bonds that at some point give the bearer the option of converting the bonds into shares of stock. Because this is usually a desirable situation, the interest rates on convertible bonds tend to be lower than on similar bonds without the convertible option. Convertible bonds are generally pretty confusing to the diversification of a portfolio because the balance between bonds and stocks is one of the key aspects of diversification. When bonds can suddenly turn into stocks, you've got a diversification mess on your hands. Still, convertibles are attractive for those who wouldn't mind ending up with part ownership of the issuing company.

Corporate bonds can be purchased directly from the issuer (actually, from the investment banks that underwrite the bonds being issued), but are more commonly purchased on the open market either in fund form or from a broker. More on this later.

Other Bond Types

So far we have talked about bonds issued by the US government and US corporations. But of course there are also bonds from governments and companies around the world. From the perspective of a US investor, these latter offerings are generally just called foreign corporate bonds. Bonds issued by the governments of the world, called *sovereign bonds*, fall into three categories: *mature market, emerging market, and frontier* bonds. Mature market bonds come from large, stable, established governments (such as Canada, Germany, and Japan). Emerging market bonds are those issued by the governments of smaller countries with poorer economies. Frontier bonds come from the smallest and poorest countries.

An additional wrinkle is the currency in which foreign bonds are denominated. Bonds issued by foreign companies or governments that are denominated in US dollars are called *Yankee bonds*. Yankee bonds come without the need of a currency conversion, but they don't provide as much market diversification in your portfolio as do bonds that are denominated in other currencies. Most emerging market and frontier bonds are denominated in US dollars, while most mature international governments issue bonds in their own currencies.

Beyond these international bonds, there are many other types of individual bonds (issued by churches, charities, and social activist groups, to name just a few). None of that complexity is worth examining here, a fact the reader will likely appreciate at this point.

Stocks (also known as Equities)

A share of stock in a company confers to the bearer a little slice of ownership in that company. People buy stocks in order to gain financially in two ways:

1. Dividends
2. Capital gains

Dividends are portions of the profits of a company that are paid out to shareholders on a per share basis. *Capital gains* result from the increase of the price of a stock above the price for which the bearer purchased it.

There are two types of capital gains. A *paper capital gain* means your stock has gone up in value, but you haven't yet sold it; therefore, you only have the gain "on paper." This is important because US tax laws do not tax paper gains for individual investors. As long as you hold the stock, you receive the gain from an increased price in that stock without having to *yet* pay any tax on it. As we will see later, this is an important incentive to maintain a long-term buy-and-hold strategy for stock investing.

A *realized gain* is one that results from selling a stock that has gone up in value. Realized capital gains are subject to federal taxation. Now, when it comes to capital gains taxes, there are two time frames: *short-term* capital gains and *long-term* capital gains. These two types of capital gains are taxed at different rates.

Short-term capital gains (those that resulted from buying and selling a stock in one year or less) are taxed as ordinary income, meaning they are taxed at your regular federal income tax rate. Long-term capital gains are treated much more kindly, as the capital gains tax rate is much less than ordinary income tax rates. See the chart below:

US Tax Rate from 2013 onward

Ordinary Income Tax Rate	Long-term Capital Gains Tax Rate
10%	0%
15%	0%
25%	15%
28%	15%
33%	15%
35%	15%
39.6%	20%

Simply find your federal tax rate in the left hand column, and that will be the amount you'll pay in taxes on any *short-term* capital gains. Look across to the corresponding number in the right column, and you'll find the percentage tax you'll pay on *long-term* capital gains. At every level of taxation, it benefits the individual to hold her stocks and realize her capital gain over the course of at least a year and one day.

Market Capitalization

The next thing to know about stock investing is that something called market capitalization has a big effect on the value of a particular stock. It is also important when attempting to diversify your portfolio. Market capitalization is the total amount of value represented by multiplying the price of a share of stock by the number of shares outstanding. So if a company had one million shares of stock out there at $10 per share, their market capitalization would be $10 million.

Based on a company's market capitalization, investors will classify it in one of several categories:

- **Micro Cap** (which stands for micro-capitalization) is for stocks from the smallest companies. Generally this range is taken to be for companies with a market capitalization of less than $250 million.
- **Small Cap** is for stocks of companies with a market capitalization between $250 million to $1 billion.
- **Mid Cap** is for market capitalizations of between $1 billion and $10 billion.
- **Large Cap** runs between $10 billion and $50 billion.
- **Ultra Cap** represents anything above $50 billion.

The micro cap and ultra cap terms are sometimes not used, in which case you will usually just hear about small, mid, and large cap stocks. These are just general guidelines, but they give a pretty good indication as to the size of the entity represented by the stock.

Growth versus Income

There is another way of looking at stocks. Investors say a stock is either a growth stock or an income stock. They consider *growth stocks* to be equities from those companies that have the potential to outgrow the market in general, will devote most of their profits toward reinvestment in future growth, and are in a fast-growing or high-potential industry or sector. Growth stocks usually don't pay any dividends at all. Therefore, investors in growth stocks expect to sell them at a higher price (and hence a profit) at some point in the future.

Income stocks are those that are usually from very sturdy, well-established companies that pay large dividend yields. Investors pick up these stocks not so much to see them rise in price as to reap the ongoing large dividend payouts. The goal is to find dividend yields that exceed what an investor can find in the bond market.

Stock Exchanges and Brokerages

Stocks of publicly traded companies are easily bought and sold. This is because there are many good *stock markets* or *stock exchanges* around the world on which particular stocks are "listed." For instance, General Electric (symbol GE) is listed on the New York Stock Exchange. Some exchanges are entirely electronic, while others still maintain some form of a physical trading floor. This has very little effect on the stock investor, however, as he or she will work with a *broker* who is authorized by the exchanges to execute trades of the stocks in question.

Usually, an individual investor will establish a brokerage account (similar to a bank account) with a particular brokerage firm. There are full-service and discount brokerage firms, as well as online brokerage firms. Full-service firms charge higher commissions for each trade they execute on your behalf, but they also offer investment ideas and advice. Discount brokerages offer fewer of these services and usually have lower commissions and fees. Online brokerages are usually the cheapest, offer no real person-to-person investing advice, but do usually provide great research tools and data for a wide range of investment vehicles.

In general, the concept is to keep your costs as low as possible, because even small ongoing costs can add up to a huge drain on your ability to compound growth forward through the years. As

John Bogle wrote, "If investors could rely on only a single factor to select future superior performers and to avoid future inferior performers, it would be fund costs. The record could hardly be clearer: *the more the managers and brokers take, the less the investors make*" (emphasis his). For this reason discount brokerage firms, and particularly those online, are dominating the field of private investing these days. The amazing amount of research, reporting, and information they make available to the individual investor would have been unheard of for even a professional just a few decades ago. This type of revolution in an industry due to the Internet is perhaps nowhere more pronounced than in the world of stock trading and investing.

Fundamental versus Technical Analysis

When it comes to stock investing, there is a great divide between two dominant strategies:

- Fundamental investing
- Technical investing

Fundamental investing is the approach to stock picking that bases its decisions upon the financial stability of the company represented by the stock. Many factors are considered in this approach, from an analysis of the company's balance sheet and income statement to the ability of its management team. Quantities such as a stock's price to earnings ratio (P/E), its price to book value (the total capitalization divided by the total assets of the company), the company's projected earnings growth, and other fundamentals are all considered as part of the determination about whether to invest in a particular stock. In the purest sense, fundamental investors are not interested in the recent price movement of the stock or the volume that has been traded. They see themselves as buying a portion of the company, and their analysis is done to indicate whether they are buying a good company or not. We spoke of Benjamin Graham and value investing earlier; he exemplifies this fundamental approach.

Technical investors are quite different. In the most extreme variety, technical analysis doesn't really concern itself with the stability or profitability of a company. It certainly doesn't try to make any judgments about the abilities of the company's management staff. Instead, technical traders get all the information they need from looking at the price and volume charts of the stock itself (among other technical indicators). They read patterns and trends and look at the performance history of the stock in question against the behavior of the markets as a whole. Specifically, they try to "time" the market by selecting the most opportune moment to buy into a trade and then find the most profitable time to bow out of it. Day traders (those who speculate in quick in-and-out trades during the course of one day or less) are often of the technical school of thought.

It is only fair for us to point out that most day traders never make any money, and technical analysis is still a black sheep in the investing world. Most of the icons of investing disregard technical analysis entirely. However, some lean toward a blend of the two approaches, citing that fundamental analysis tells an investor *what* stock to buy, and technical analysis tells her *when* to buy it. This sounds nice, but only the top experts who manage the biggest, most successful hedge funds seem able to make that strategy work with any regularity.

For the rest of us mere mortals, the relative ease with which fundamental investing over a long time frame leads to excellent returns makes it the best strategy. Still, if you would like to speculate a little bit in your stock investing (only as a hobby, and only with a portion of money you can stand to lose), then technical analysis might be fun for a while. Just be warned that trying to time the market is almost always a fool's game.

Industries and Sectors

Another way to look at the world of stocks is by knowing the sector and industry in which the company operates. A sector is the higher category, and is a group of interrelated industries. So an industry is really just a subsector.

For instance, health care is a sector. Within the health care sector are many industries such as pharmaceuticals, medical equipment, and services. Sectors and their industries (subsectors) are important to track because again, you want to diversify across different categories when building your portfolio. Being too invested in any one sector can expose your portfolio to too much acute risk. If you are heavily concentrated in the petroleum industry, and then the world hits an oil glut (as is happening at the time of this writing), then the value of your portfolio could take a real hit. Being spread out across many sectors and industries is a wise way to look at diversification.

Also there are two types of industries to consider. One is *cyclical*, and the other is *defensive*. Cyclical means that the company basically sells products and services that are merely wants and not really needs. In bad economies, these types of companies generally have a tougher time, and the price of their stock usually plummets. Defensive industries (not to be confused with *the* defense industry, as in those who supply the military) represent companies that sell us things we need all the time, whether we are in a good economy or a bad one. Therefore, their performances tend to be smoother through economic fluctuations and represent safer investments (although they don't tend to fly as high in good times as do cyclical ones).

Shorting

Buying a stock for dividends and buying it for a capital gain are not really the only two ways of making money from stocks. We made it that simple just to help you move through the material. There is also a backward way to play a stock.

When someone buys a security and hopes for a profit as a result of its price going up, that investor is said to "be long" in that stock. It means they are hoping for an upward move in the price. But the opposite can also be done. An investor can actually take on a position wherein he benefits if the stock goes down instead.

How is this done? It's called *shorting, going short,* or *selling short.* The investor borrows a stock he thinks will go down and sells it at today's price. Later, if the stock goes down, he "buys" it at the new lower price and then returns it to the original lender, pocketing the difference. So while most people are familiar with the concept of buying low and selling high, many are excited to learn that there is a way to do the opposite: sell high now and then buy low later.

However, shorting is not for everyone. And actually, it is not for many. This is because there is no limit to how much money you can lose. When "going long," all you can lose is 100 percent of the money you used to purchase the stock. When going short, you can lose way more than 100 percent of the money you invested in the transaction. Further, markets are very hard to predict, and the interest you pay to the lender of the stock while you are waiting to "close out" your short position can eat into potential profits. As John Maynard Keynes said almost a century ago, "The market can remain irrational

> **"The market can remain irrational much longer than you can remain solvent."**
> **—John Maynard Keynes**

much longer than you can remain solvent." This means that you may correctly believe that a stock is going to go down. But being right and being right at *the right time* are two different things!

While it is important for your financial education to realize that markets can be played from both sides (and that's the long and the short of it!), shorting is not recommended as a strategy unless you really want to dig deep and become an expert in individual stock investing. The proven strategies recommended by the best investment minds in history for the average individual investor like you and us are much safer, much easier, much less complicated, and much more likely to result in financial returns. It is those strategies we'll cover in chapters 8 and 9. Hang on, we're getting there!

Foreign and Emerging Market Stocks

Just as we saw with bonds, stocks are also available in almost all the same varieties. Generally, the "large cap" stocks are considered the safest, with "mid cap" and then "small cap" being a little more risky. Next, as we work our way up the Risk Meter, come foreign stocks from companies in developed nations and then the stocks from companies in emerging and frontier markets.

Of course, nothing is this neat and tidy, and risk, if you'll remember, is a relative term. Still, know that a good blend of stocks from each of these categories will help build a more diversified portfolio. We know you must be sick of us telling you that as we review each of these asset classes, but you'll thank us for already knowing it when we get to chapter 8!

Real Estate

As you already know, real estate comes in two dominant forms: *commercial* and *residential*. And much like stocks, real estate investors seek to reap money from their investment by either collecting ongoing rents or gaining capital appreciation, or by both.

As investments go, real estate is higher on the Risk Meter because it is generally very illiquid, meaning it can often be hard to get your money out of it in a timely fashion. It is often complicated, requires expensive maintenance, and is subject to a type of taxation that stocks and bonds don't have to deal with called *property tax*. This is a unique kind of tax because you have to pay an ongoing, annual tax simply because you *possess* it. Strange (imagine if they taxed stock and bond holdings in such a way), but who's to stand in the way of a government that wants some money?

So real estate has three main taxes: property taxes paid annually, regular income tax paid on rents, and capital gains taxes paid when you sell it. This is in addition to the fees and sales taxes you pay to state and local governments when you buy and sell it (again, imagine having to pay a sales tax on a stock or bond)! However, at least for one's primary residence, the interest paid on mortgage debt is tax-deductible for people below a certain income level or for those whose mortgage interest deduction takes them above the standard marital deduction.

Real estate has a special attraction for lots of investors, however, because it is one of the easiest investments to borrow money against in order to buy it. Interest rates for money lent to buy property are generally very low, and there are many neat little laws that allow a seller of one property to roll the gains made on that sale into the purchase of a bigger investment in property. Because of these types of tricks, smart real estate investors can skirt some of the many tax liabilities properties generate and also use other people's money to *leverage* large gains on small amounts of their own capital. Some investors call this kind of debt *good debt*. There is also nothing like the passive income received on an ongoing basis from tenants (either residential or commercial) paying rents.

In recent times, some creations have made the advantages of real estate even easier to access for the individual investor. These are called Real Estate Investment Trusts (or REITs). They are just what they sound like, trusts. A trust is a special-tax-situation partnership that can be made up of many individuals. When you buy a share of a REIT, you are technically becoming one of the partners in the trust. REITs own collections of real estate (such as shopping centers, amusement parks, apartment complexes, and even commercial mortgages) and pay out the proceeds to shareholders. REITs as trusts have special tax status, and as a result must pay 90 percent of their income as dividends to shareholders. For this reason the cash flow from REITs is very good and offers a yield much higher than even the highest dividend-paying stocks.

REITs are nice because the individual holder of shares in a REIT does not have to mess around with hiring property managers, getting appraisals, securing loans, or any of the usually messy stuff associated with buying and owning property. One doesn't even have to fix toilets! REITs can be purchased through a broker just as simply as stocks or bonds. Further, REITs allow a much larger diversification than would otherwise be available to an individual. The average REIT holds hundreds of properties, usually across a broad spectrum of geography or type. This offers great diversification (you knew we would get to that eventually) and exposure to an asset class that doesn't correlate in its price movements to many of the other classes, such as stocks and bonds.

The downside of REITs is their tax implications. REITs themselves do not have to pay any income tax; instead, the burden for this is passed along to shareholders. These dividends are taxed as ordinary income for the shareholder in an REIT. For that reason they are best held within a tax advantaged account such as a 401(k) or IRA.

**Commodities, Futures, Options,
Derivatives, Currencies, Etc.**

Okay, if you're still with us, you may be thinking this chapter could go on forever—and it could! We haven't yet touched on commodities, futures, options, and the huge array of derivatives that are all available to the individual investor. Oh, and don't forget currencies! Suffice it to say that these are all very high level investments that aren't suitable to the individual investor without a lot of education and practice first, which is beyond the scope of this book. These investment vehicles are usually more risky and complicated than anything we've discussed to this point. We would highly recommend gaining experience with the classes we've covered so far before venturing into these areas as an investor. Still, a lot can be accomplished with these vehicles, and it's not necessary to simply dismiss them outright. As you grow in financial stature and experience, you may be well served by walking into these waters. But you'll need a book beyond this one in order to do so!

Angel Investing and Venture Capital

There are even riskier investments than we have yet discussed. These have one thing in common: they all involve direct investment of money in a business enterprise over which the investor has no direct control. In other words, this is money you put directly into a business *someone else* is starting, not you.

There are risks with starting any business, of course, but when you are in control of it yourself, the risks to your money are lower because you are at the helm. No one will more carefully deploy or more fiercely guard those precious funds than you, the person who is utilizing them. When you are putting money in *someone else's* business, you can't be so sure.

One form of direct investing in someone's business idea is through seed capital or *angel investing*. This occurs at a very early stage in the business's life. For a certain percentage of ownership in the company, you throw in your money and pray for the best. Sure, you can advise those running the business, but this isn't usually part of the deal. You put in your money, they use it to build up their firm, and down the road, at an unspecified time, you supposedly get not only your original money back but some great growth in the value of your percentage of ownership because the company has taken off and gotten profitable. Do we really need to tell you how rare an occurrence this is? The odds are so low of making any money as an angel investor that it might be better for you just to fly to Vegas and play slot machines blindly. Still, often the person asking you for an angel investment is a friend or relative, and these can be some of the most difficult to turn down.

Venture capital is the money that flows into a new enterprise once a basic level of viability (using angel/seed funds first) has been established. Venture capital is usually professional money provided by a firm funded by a group of wealthy investors who are willing to run the risk of long odds to occasionally hit one out of the park by, for instance, funding the next Facebook. You may have an occasion, especially once you move beyond financial fitness, to participate with a group of venture capitalists. If so, you should still realize that most of these deals also don't pan out. The principle is to never invest money at these high, risky levels that you cannot afford to lose entirely.

Art, Jewelry, Gems, Collectibles

We finish with a final group of investment possibilities, which includes art, jewelry, gems, and collectibles. We have now come to the very top of the Risk Meter. These are pretty much the most speculative possibilities available to the individual investor.

Fine art is an interesting investment class, because it *does* seem that at the highest level, art holds its value like almost nothing else. In times of war and even depression, the world's most treasured art has held its value and found high price buyers without much interruption. Of course, this is a rich person's game, as the paintings and pieces to which we are referring are worth millions and millions of dollars each. Perhaps someday, when you progress far beyond mere financial fitness, you can acquire some of the world's art treasures and be extremely confident that your wealth will thereby be preserved. As for the art that doesn't necessarily fit into this top category, your chances of losing money increase exponentially. At these levels there are so many subjective judgments that unless you become an art expert, you are likely to get burned.

Jewelry is, if possible, even more speculative than art. There are several categories of jewelry, from the new fashionable designs to those pieces with historical significance. But the market for the finest jewelry is very small, and jewelry as an investment class has not always held its value very well. When times get tough, one of the first things people hock is their jewelry. For this reason jewelry values swing wildly with the economy, which means that just when you may need to sell off some pieces of your own, thousands of other people will be liquidating theirs as well. It is much better to confine your jewelry purchases to romantic and family uses, without trying to consider it an actual investment. One possible exception to this would be men's watches. There are a few handcrafted watches, made for generations by (usually) Swiss companies, that seem to hold their value almost as well as fine art. The leader in this category is Patek Philippe, which guarantees its watches forever. Patek Philippes have been known to hit valuations in the millions of dollars. Some of the super-rich use them to move wealth across international borders, pass it along to future generations, and otherwise hide it in plain sight.

Gems are close cousins to jewelry, and with very rare exception, all the same warnings apply. Diamonds, in particular, are falsely valued in the marketplace, because the supply is artificially limited in order to keep retail prices high. Overall, don't fool yourself into thinking you are "investing" when being talked into buying an expensive piece of jewelry or some supposedly valuable stones. Unless you really know what you're doing, you are likely to "buy dear and sell fear."[3] The last of these miscellaneous investment classes we'll consider is *collectibles*. Some people get really involved in this and put huge sums of money into rare coins or autographed jerseys and the like. Again, the market is so specialized in these areas and so small that if you ever really needed to sell your collections, you'd find it difficult to get the prices you wanted unless you happened to time the market just right. Also, success in these categories requires a great deal of specialized knowledge. Therefore, if you decide to put some money into collectibles, consider it an enjoyable hobby and not a serious investment strategy. And as always, at this high level of risk, put in no money you cannot afford to lose.

Summary

We've been through quite a lot in this chapter, and believe it or not, we've merely viewed the tips of the proverbial icebergs! For each of the asset classes we've explored, there are many more things to know. One could literally spend a lifetime becoming an

---

3 This comes from the trite investing jingle that says to buy when others are in fear and sell when others find it dear, or the more recent variant, "buy from fear and sell into greed."

expert in any one of these categories. However, that is not our purpose here. What we set out to do was familiarize you with the broad array of asset classes available to the individual investor and give you at least an introductory knowledge of each. Hopefully we've accomplished that. Our second purpose was to help you realize that unless you have a lifetime to dedicate to becoming an investing expert yourself, you will likely get burned in the market by those who do.

So what is the individual investor with a life of her own to do? How can one make sense of this enormous landscape of investment possibilities without expending all one's time and energy? What can one do to take advantage of all the possibilities without drowning in the complexities? Fortunately, many of the greatest investment minds of all time have developed strategies that are easy to implement and take advantage of the majority of the gains to be had from these markets, all the while protecting against loss. Ultimately, these titans of the money world have constructed some shortcuts. It's these shortcuts that comprise the right side of the Risk Meter, which we'll turn to next.

SEVEN

Assets Explained – Part II The Right Side of the Risk Meter

"The intelligent investor will minimize to the bare bones the costs of financial intermediation. That's what common sense tells us. That's what indexing is all about."
—JOHN C. BOGLE

In the last chapter we reviewed the full spectrum of assets available to the individual investor. This chapter will seek to explain the shortcuts that have been developed to provide easier access to many of those asset classes. As with the specific assets themselves, some of the vehicles we'll discuss in this chapter are riskier than others. But really, there is a huge amount of overlap, and the risk has more to do with the asset class than with the type of shortcut vehicles we'll be analyzing here. So the order below is not that important.

Mutual Funds

Every now and then someone comes along with a great idea. One of the greatest financial inventions of the twentieth century (which actually had its start in the Netherlands back in 1774 but only really gained a footing during the "Roaring Twenties") has to be the *mutual fund*. A mutual fund, at its most basic level, is a pool of money from individual investors placed into a particular group of assets and looked after by a professional.

There is actually a lot more to it than that, which we'll get to in a moment, but the beauty of a mutual fund is the access it gives the individual investor to a broad array of assets. Through a mutual fund one can own portions of companies, hold baskets of bonds, or invest in real estate (remember the REITs from the previous chapter?) without having to research, select, and purchase them directly and individually. Instead, one can just submit money to the desired fund and let the professionals do the rest. This provides convenience, diversification, and liquidity, as the money in a mutual fund is generally almost immediately redeemable. It also allows an investor with only modest means access to small slivers of many different assets, none of which he could afford individually.

The mutual fund industry is now enormous. It is estimated that more than $15 trillion is held in approximately 8,000 different funds. The variety available is also staggering, offering investors everything from bonds and stocks to real estate and money markets. There are magazines and websites dedicated to providing performance data for mutual funds, and fund managers who have a good year (meaning their investments of the funds they oversee in their particular fund outperform the rest of the market as a whole) become rock stars. If a fund manager has a good year or two, investors flock to that fund in droves, pouring money in and dramatically increasing the size of the fund.

If mutual funds get too big, they can close their doors to new investors. This may seem strange, since having more money and investors means more fees and income for the manager and her company. But when a fund gets too large, it becomes harder to move that amount of money around effectively and can actually hurt the fund's annual performance. So sometimes the best funds aren't available to new investors. Or they will raise the minimum dollar amount required for new accounts.

There are two predominant types of mutual funds: closed-end funds and open-end funds. *Closed-end funds* are not as popular today as they once were. They offer a fixed amount of shares when they launch, and don't allow anyone new to invest their money in the fund once it's open. The only way to get involved is to buy shares from someone who already owns them. Generally, closed-end funds exist for a set time and then close down, liquidating their entire holdings back to the fund's shareholders. *Open-end funds* make up most of the market today. An open-end fund usually remains open in perpetuity and generally has no limit on the amount of new investors allowed to put their money into the fund.

Mutual funds trade once per day, meaning the custodian of the fund sets their price after the markets close each day. The way to invest is to fill out a form, usually online, that allows you to open an account directly with one of the many fund providers or through a brokerage account that gives you access to the funds of more than one company. There are then several ways to invest your money in either a lump sum or predetermined amounts over time.

All of this may sound quite appealing about now, given the simplification that mutual funds provide compared to the complexity and variety of asset classes we examined in the last chapter. At this point, the reader might be thinking that, thanks to mutual funds, investing is now a simple matter of checking out which funds have performed the best in the past and putting one's money there. That would match the thinking of millions of individual investors, and it would even follow the advice of many advisers.

But simply pouring your money into mutual funds now would cost you enormous amounts over the course of your lifetime.

You see, a huge controversy rages in the mutual fund world. It is centered upon the two different strategic approaches to managing a mutual fund.

The strategy that began the mutual fund industry, which still dominates the advertising and financial press for mutual funds today, is called *active management*. Active management seeks to outperform the market by making strategic trades with the fund's money. The managers may think a certain sector of stocks is going to be hot this year, so they dump many of the holdings in the fund from the prior year and buy heavily into that sector. Or they may think a market dip is coming, so they liquidate stocks and buy bonds. Many mutual funds will advertise their "style," or overall approach, which usually spells out the asset classes in which they will predominantly trade, and they try to confine themselves to those parameters. Active management promises the mutual fund investor that an expert will handle her funds in the most strategic way. This involves choosing the right sectors, the right securities, and the right timing. The key word here is *active*, meaning that a lot of trading activity will be taking place in the attempt to maximize the return of the fund.

The other management strategy for mutual funds is called *passive management*. This is done through a type of mutual fund called an *index fund*. An index fund sets itself up to merely invest directly in the assets represented by a particular index, such as the S&P 500, *and then do nothing further*. Slight adjustments may have to be made periodically in the holdings of the fund to make sure it continues to match the proportion of the securities in the particular index (depending upon the type of index), but other than that, the fund is entirely passive, with no ongoing trading. An index fund, therefore, delivers the same return as the index. There is no hype, no advertising, and no high-profile money manager at the helm.

Just what, then, is the controversy between actively managed funds and passive funds? It all began with a senior thesis at Princeton by a guy named John C. Bogle, whom we've already quoted. His analysis of the mutual fund industry found something shocking. Despite all the hype about active management and stellar returns by financial experts running mutual funds, the truth was that they were costing individual investors a lot of money. The constant trading in an attempt to beat the market results in a litany of costs. These include up-front sales charges and "loads," management fees, operating expenses, brokerage commissions, the invisible costs in the bid-ask spreads, market impact costs, opportunity costs if money goes into one sector while another does well instead, and finally the big one: taxes on realized gains from all those trades. Bogle's research indicated, as Benjamin Graham had theorized before, that a simple mutual fund invested in an index would, over time, outperform actively traded funds. So in 1974 Bogle launched the Vanguard Group and in 1975 opened the first index fund (today known as the Vanguard 500 Index Fund).

Because the emergence of low-cost index funds threatens the status quo of thousands of money managers and a whole host of "middlemen and -women" making money off of investors, they remain controversial. But this really shouldn't be. The argument is over. The data is in. The facts speak for themselves. And the experts (at least the ones who don't stand to make money from actively managed funds) agree.

First of all, remember what we said early in this book: that very few people can "beat the market," and almost nobody can do it consistently. According to Jack R. Meyer, former president of Harvard Management Company, who tripled the Harvard endowment from $8 billion to $27 billion, "The investment business is a giant scam. Most people think they can find managers who can outperform, but most people are wrong. I will say that

85 to 90 percent of managers fail to match their benchmarks. Because managers have fees and incur transaction costs, you know that in the aggregate they are deleting value."

Second, because of the active trading of managed mutual funds, as that quote from Meyer just indicated, the costs eat into what gets compounded over time. John C. Bogle himself stated, "Investors pay far too little attention to the cost of investing. [There is a] truly confiscatory impact of cost over an investment lifetime. In the investment field, time doesn't heal all wounds. It makes them worse. Where returns are concerned, time is your friend. But where costs are concerned, time is your enemy . . . . [Over] the long term, the miracle of compounding *returns* is overwhelmed by the tyranny of compounding *costs*" (emphasis his).

> "In the investment field, time doesn't heal all wounds. It makes them worse. Where returns are concerned, time is your friend. But where costs are concerned, time is your enemy."
> —John C. Bogle

In short, the cost of actively traded mutual funds over time eats up enormous amounts of wealth, which the passively managed index fund would have preserved for the investor. When these costs are then compounded over time, the results are devastating. There are endless statistics available to back up the claims of these experts, but we'll use just one, which will be sufficient. In the period from 1980 through 2005, a $10,000 initial investment in an index fund grew by a remarkable $178,800, compared with growth of just $98,200 in the average actively traded mutual fund. *The actively managed funds, run by market experts, amounted to only 57 percent of the total accumulation from the index fund!* If we stated those numbers in real terms (meaning accounting for inflation), the gap in performance of the index fund over the actively managed fund would be even wider! David Swensen wrote, "The mutual fund industry is a co-lossal failure . . . resulting from its systematic exploitation of in-dividual investors . . . as funds extract enormous sums from in-vestors in exchange for providing a shocking disservice . . . ."

In short, it would be a shame to fight your way out of the Financial Matrix only to fall prey to an In-vestment Matrix! Remember the analogy from the film, *The Matrix*? That a whole system existed to exploit people who weren't even aware of it? Much the same sce-nario can be seen at work in the investment world. Advertisements, "talking-head" chatter on television, articles in the *Wall Street Journal*, and investing news-letters all feed into the myth that actively managed mutual funds are good for the individual investor. It's an Investment Matrix!

> **In short, it would be a shame to fight your way out of the Financial Matrix only to fall prey to an Investment Matrix.**

As you grow in your financial stature and have more money available to invest in a growing portfolio of assets, be sure to pay careful attention to the costs of doing so. Never forget that even small costs can be a killer when compounded over time. And if you are considering investing in mutual funds, stick with low cost index funds with the smallest operating expenses.

> **Never forget that even small costs can be a killer when compounded over time.**

Again, however, don't take it from us. One of the most suc-cessful hedge fund managers of all time, Clifford S. Asness, said the following: "Market-cap based indexing will never be driven from its deserved perch as core and deserved king of the invest-ment world. It is what we should all own . . . and it has delivered low-cost equity returns to a great mass of investors . . . the now and forever king-of-the-hill." Princeton University professor and best-selling investment researcher Burton Malkiel wrote, "The point is that it is highly unlikely you can beat the market. It is so rare that it's like looking for a needle in a haystack. A strategy far more likely to be optimal is to buy the haystack itself: that is, buy an index fund . . . ." And none other than the famous Peter Lynch, who himself was able to outperform the market for years, stated, "The public would be better off in an index fund."

> "The point is that it is highly unlikely you can beat the market. It is so rare that it's like looking for a needle in a haystack. A strategy far more likely to be optimal is to buy the haystack itself: that is, buy an index fund."
> —Burton Malkiel

So by all means take advantage of the convenience and diversification provided by mutual funds. But be sure to do so in the most cost-effective, positively compounding manner: by owning low-cost market-cap index funds. As for which ones to own, and in what proportion, we'll get to that in the next chapter.

Exchange-Traded Funds (ETFs)

But don't rush to buy index mutual funds just yet, because there's yet one more nuance we'd like to share with you. One good idea often leads to another, and somewhere along the way (actually, on the Toronto Stock Exchange) the concept of mutual funds that trade like stocks got proposed. What resulted is the massive market of what are known as *Exchange-Traded Funds*, or ETFs. First appearing in the early 1990s, ETFs are a hybrid between a mutual fund and a stock. Initially catching fire with big institutions because of the ease with which larger amounts of money can be moved around using this type of trading mechanism, ETFs are now gaining popularity with individual investors, too, and for good reason. Accounting for several trillion dollars of investment in the marketplace so far, they are a fast-growing method of accessing all the good things mutual funds offer but in a more effective manner.

First of all, ETFs are not traded once per day after the market closes as mutual funds are (where special deals can occur away from the eyes of the public, or where large institutions get better pricing than do individuals); rather, ETFs trade throughout the day on exchanges in plain sight of everyone. Also, ETFs are closely regulated by the US Securities and Exchange Commission. But there are many features that distinguish an ETF from a mutual fund, and many of these are clear-cut advantages:

1. ETFs are bought and sold like stocks (as we said), and as with stocks, ETF trading usually requires the payment of a brokerage commission (though many brokerage houses are now offering hundreds of ETFs commission free).

2. Also like stocks, ETFs can be bought and sold with *limit*, *market*, and *stop-loss* orders (these are helpful tools used in giving brokers directions on how and when you want to buy in or sell out of a particular stock or ETF; this type of specificity is run-of-the-mill for stock trading but not otherwise available with mutual funds).

3. ETFs tend to represent index funds, which we saw in the preceding section have enormous advantages over actively managed funds.

4. ETFs cost less than mutual funds (even for the same exact fund, as many mutual funds are available in both conventional mutual fund form and also as ETF—which have a lower expense ratio because their costs are so much less due to brokerage houses handling most of the paperwork related to those investing in them).

5. ETFs result in less in taxable capital gains for their investors, partly because they mostly follow indexes. But there is another reason, and it's one of the biggest advantages an ETF has over a mutual fund. When someone wants his money sent back out of a mutual fund, the fund is forced to sell in order to free up cash to do so. This causes *realized capital gains* for the fund. But when someone wants out of an ETF, all they have to do is sell their shares to another willing buyer, causing no changes in the holdings of the ETF itself. This is huge, because you, the individual investor who chooses to hold on to his shares in an ETF, don't get hit with capital gains taxes just because *others* chose to sell out (as would happen if you were holding on to a mutual fund). For this reason alone ETFs are a better deal than mutual funds.

6. ETFs have no minimum investment amounts, unlike many mutual funds, so you can buy in at an extremely small price, in effect buying just one "share" of a particular ETF if you so desire

7. ETFs can be "shorted" just like a stock, thereby giving you the chance to play the "other side of the market." (Remember that this is dangerous, though, and should only be done with caution.)

8. All ETF transactions are public and therefore more transparent than mutual funds.

9. ETFs, because they are bought and sold like stocks, don't require cash to be sitting on hand as do mutual funds, which must be able to immediately fulfill redemptions of investors who want their money out of the fund. This is a huge difference between the two, and it means ETFs won't have some percentage of their holdings losing out on market movements. Instead, ETFs will be *all in*, all the time, not missing out on upward trends in the market

because some of their investors' money is sitting on the sidelines.

10. An individual investor can own a large collection of ETFs in one place at one brokerage house, providing great possibilities for diversification.

11. ETFs can be bought and sold *on margin* (meaning you can borrow money from the brokerage house to invest even more heavily in ETFs than the money you have of your own in the brokerage account; this is very risky, however).

12. ETFs can also be traded on the *options* markets. We skipped over options in the last chapter, but these give the ETF investor a lot of options (pun unavoidable!) for hedging his investment position, if so desired. Again, this is not available with mutual fund investing.

Again, not all of these are necessarily recommended, but just a quick glance at this list demonstrates the many features of ETFs that are not available with mutual funds.

Interestingly, one of the biggest promoters of ETFs is Vanguard, the same company that pioneered index funds. According to financial advisor Russell Wild, "This ain't rocket science. For most buy-and-hold investors, ETFs will almost always be the better choice [than mutual funds], at least in the long run."

We would be remiss, however, if we didn't offer up some warnings about ETFs. As you may have guessed by now, there is always "the other side of the story" when it comes to investing. All the advantages of ETFs as described above come crashing down if you use them improperly.

The first warning is this: ETFs are easy to trade, but that doesn't mean that they *should* be. Don't get sucked into buying and selling or trying to time the markets or chase returns. Be careful, because many online brokerage services even offer "commission free trades" of ETFs, which is wonderful for the buy-and-hold investor but is also a temptation to the less disciplined investor to churn his own account with buying and selling. Don't fall for it, or you'll obliterate all the advantages of index investing that ETFs make so attractive.

The second warning is that more and more ETFs are being constructed that are *not* true index funds. Instead, either they are actively managed, or they are based on indices that aren't proper indices[1] and therefore require the fund manager to actively manage the money. This leads to higher operating costs and all the disadvantages of actively managed mutual funds.

In short, proper index fund ETFs provide the lowest-cost, most tax-efficient way for an individual investor to access diverse securities across various types and markets. Used properly, meaning when used as part of a long-term buy-and-hold strategy, they provide all the advantages that originally made mutual funds so popular while eliminating many of mutual funds' biggest weaknesses. In the next chapter, we'll dig into some exciting ways for you to use index ETFs to build a winning portfolio.

401(k)s, 403(b)s, and 457(b)s

As if the massive growth of the mutual fund industry weren't enough, the US government gave the whole concept a boost when in 1974 it passed the Employee Retirement Income Security Act. Known by its acronym, ERISA, this law effectively ushered the middle class into the stock and bond markets. Suddenly, hundreds of billions of dollars were flowing into the markets previously occupied only by professionals and the occasional individual hobby investor.

---

1 A "proper" index to follow, according to John Bogle, is a market capitalization weighted index, which attributes each of its components based on their market capitalization. This weighs larger capitalized companies in the index according to their overall capitalization size.

After the Industrial Revolution and prior to ERISA, most employees of decent-sized corporations and up were provided something called a *defined benefit plan* for their retirements. These, more commonly known as pension plans, basically promised a certain amount of ongoing pay to a retired employee based upon a formula tied to that employee's length of service and pay range at retirement. While nice for the employees, these obligations grew expensive for the companies providing them (and outside of those being provided by federal, state, and local governments to their employees, pension plans are nearly extinct today). Further, not all companies were sizable enough to provide these benefits, and many employees were left without.

Enter ERISA, which created the *defined contribution plan*. Under ERISA, the employee regularly puts her *own* money away toward retirement, with the company often matching with a small corresponding contribution of its own. As you may have guessed, these are more popularly referred to as 401(k)s—and 403(b)s for employees of tax-exempt organizations and 457(b)s for government employees. Suddenly, millions of middle-class employees were contributing their own money toward their retirements, and most of that money was flowing directly into the very convenient mutual fund industry.

The first concept of a 401(k)—we'll stop also referring to 403(b)s and 457(b)s here, but know that we mean all three—was that the employee herself was responsible for kicking in money throughout her career to fund her own retirement. Compared to the defined benefit plans that went before, this was a radical shift. But the second big concept was the idea of *tax deferral*. Tax deferral allows two benefits:

1. The employee's payments made into such an account come out of her pay *before* taxes are assessed, thereby reducing her taxable income during the years of contribution; and

2. The payments accumulate and grow tax-free inside the fund, with taxes on that growth deferred until the time funds are taken out.

This meant that you were encouraged to contribute money into a 401(k) plan because it would lower your tax burden now and because your investment could grow unimpeded by taxes throughout the years. The idea was that you wouldn't be taxed on the gains until much later, when you would be retiring, getting rid of your primary income, and thereby most likely operating at a much lower tax rate.

The tax laws discourage you from taking your money out of a 401(k) until you are at least 59½ years of age. If you do, not only will you be hit with a 10 percent penalty on the amount you withdraw, but also you will have to pay capital gains taxes on the amount of appreciation attributed to your withdrawal. Neither of these is a good idea. So ultimately, you want to leave your 401(k) alone until you are the proper age.

However, there are some exceptions for hardships, which include the following:

1. Medical expenses
2. College tuition
3. Being evicted from your home
4. Funeral expenses
5. Damage to your principal residence

In each of these cases there are rules as to what constitutes a true hardship, and in order to make such a withdrawal, you'll need to prove to your employer that the hardship exists. Or you can "self-certify" that you have the financial need, which keeps you from having to divulge your private financial information to your employer. However, after having made a hardship withdrawal, you will not be able to contribute further funds into your 401(k) for six months.

There are also some penalty-free reasons to withdraw money from your 401(k) before you reach the age of 59½, but such withdrawals will still be taxable. These include a qualifying disability, certain medical expenses, and a disaster for which you've been granted relief by the IRS; another reason is that you have left the company and have set up a schedule to withdraw the payments for at least five years. Each of these carries rules and restrictions, and it is best to contact your human resources department to find out the particulars for your case.

Another aspect to 401(k) programs that you should be aware of are the *required minimum distributions* (RMDs). These state that at the time you reach the age of 70½ years, you are *required* to start taking withdrawals out of your 401(k), whether you wish to or not. The amount you must begin taking out periodically is calculated based upon your life expectancy, because the federal government wants its taxes on the gains you've earned in that account all these years. You have no choice but to begin liquidating this investment.

Roth

The entire edifice of defined contribution plans was built on the concept of tax deferral—putting off the taxes on the growth in your account until way down the road when your tax rate would be expected to be lower. However, as part of the Taxpayer Relief Act of 1997, Senator William Roth Jr. from Delaware and his colleagues included in the bill something that has come to be known as the *Roth IRA* (and its sister, the *Roth 401(k)*). Basically, these work the same as what we've just described, but the assumption about a lower tax rate later in your life is cast away. The idea is that one can never know what the government will do with taxes in the future, and it is more likely than not, given the growth in our government and its spending, that taxes will rise considerably. Further, there is no predicting your own growth in earning power, and there is nothing to say that you will necessarily be at a lower tax bracket upon retirement. What if, for instance, you build up a growing personal business and thereby develop an additional stream of income that eclipses the one you get from your job or career? If you follow the principles of offense in the *Financial Fitness* book, this is a distinct possibility!

So the Roth 401(k) and Roth IRA (we'll discuss IRAs in a moment) are basically the opposite of regular 401(k)s and IRAs. Instead of the money being put away *before* it gets taxed, you contribute *after*-tax money. This means that you take some of your take-home pay and contribute it to a Roth account. Then the *growth* in that account occurs tax-free, and you *never have to pay taxes on it* at all. Further, Roth 401(k)s and IRAs have no required minimum distributions! This means that *you don't have to take the money out at any time* until you want to—or until the death of the owner of the account (and even then your heirs don't have to do it all at once). These are enormous advantages over a "regular" 401(k) or IRA, and therefore Roth plans have gotten very popular.

There are limits on how much money you can contribute annually to these plans, however. These limits are always changing, but at the time of this writing they are as follows:

For Roth 401(k), 403(b), and most 457 plans:

Age 49 and under	$18,000
Age 50 and older	$18,000 plus an additional "catch up" $6,000

For Roth and traditional IRA contributions:

Age 49 and under   Up to $5,500

Age 50 and older $5,500 plus an additional
                          "catch up" $1,000

Finally, there are income level restrictions on who can participate in these plans. Alas, if you make too much money, you are not allowed to play.

Individual Retirement Accounts (IRAs)

Individual retirement accounts or IRAs work similarly to 401(k)s above, except that they are not provided by your employer. You would approach a brokerage, bank, or life insurance company to set one up, and to be eligible you are required to earn an income. The types of investments you can put your money into inside an IRA are diverse, more so usually than what are available in most 401(k)s, including stocks, bonds, mutual funds, REITs, money market accounts, and certificates of deposit. For the most part, contributions to IRAs are not payroll deducted and therefore do not come out "pretax" as in the case with 401(k)s, but rather the contributor to an IRA would make investments manually and then deduct the contributed amount from his or her taxable income. Obviously, in the case of IRAs, there would be no employer matching contributions, as is sometimes the case with 401(k)s. IRAs also have required minimum distributions as we discussed for 401(k)s.

There are actually eleven different types of IRAs—too much to go into here! But if you don't have access to a 401(k), and if you don't make too much money, an IRA is a good way to get a tax-advantaged investment growing and could be a valuable part of your portfolio.

There are also Roth IRAs, as we covered above, and the advantages of contributing after-tax money that grows tax-free and can be taken out tax-free are significant. Again, get competent counsel for your particular situation, but in general, Roth IRAs make a lot of sense for those who are qualified to have them.

Hedge Funds

One final investment shortcut we'll touch on briefly is called a hedge fund. Mysterious, mammoth, and often misunderstood, hedge funds are lightly regulated limited partnerships that entrust large amounts of money to investing specialists. These specialists use very sophisticated investment techniques including hedging, shorting, high margin leverage, program trading, high-speed trading, currency speculation, and a whole array of sophisticated approaches to delivering large annual returns. Usually, the money is locked into place for at least a year at a time, sometimes more, and the exact investment details are kept even from the investors themselves.

Hedge funds are not open to the general public as are mutual funds; they are rarely advertised and generally don't even have websites. The only individuals who can participate in hedge fund investing are what the Securities and Exchange Commission calls *accredited investors*. These are high net-worth people with an annual income of $200,000 or more ($300,000 or more for a married couple). The other type of eligible investor is called a *qualified investor*, which is an individual, trust account, or institution with at least $5 million of investable assets. When you invest in a hedge fund, you actually sign on as a limited partner.

Some hedge funds mysteriously "beat the market" year after year. But usually, these high-profile celebrities do not accept new investing partners, and the average individual investor is left to watch in wonder from the sidelines. However, at some point in your future when you progress far beyond financial fitness, you may find it appropriate to invest in a hedge fund. By then you won't need us to tell you to be careful and do your due diligence first!

Other Countries - Many of the investment shortcuts discussed in this chapter are specific to the tax laws of the United States. Omitting them would have given a very incomplete look at the total investing landscape. However, to have included them here as we have means we risk alienating our loyal readers in other countries. Know that we included such detail here only because many of these programs have their twins in other nations, and it is our hope that by reading through this quick summary you will have at least become smarter about finding similar tax-advantaged situations for yourself based upon your particular nation's laws.

EIGHT

Diversification and Asset Allocation

*"Markets are not always or even usually correct.
But no one person or institution consistently knows
more than the market."*
—Burton G. Malkiel

It may be helpful at this point to furnish a reminder to the reader: your goose that lays the golden eggs is *you!* Your number-one investment is, and always will be, *you.* Your career, your education, your development, and whatever business or career you pursue is your number-one focus. Into that you should pour every dime you possibly can.

Now we don't recommend wasting money in any way, as money should always be stewarded properly and squeezed into its most effective use in every application. What we mean is that you should never hesitate to invest more into what you do if it can in any way advance your results. Remember, investing in you is your

> **You should never hesitate to invest more into what you do if it can in any way advance your results.**

main strategy for going *beyond* financial fitness. All the asset classes and investment possibilities we've been discussing are what you do with the money that is left over *after* you've maxed out your investment in yourself (and after you've gotten out of consumer debt).

Just know that if you maximize your investment in yourself, your career, your business, or whatever you set your hand to, there should at some point begin to be a surplus. And eventually, it is likely this surplus will begin to grow quite nicely. It is that surplus that should then be properly stewarded into further growing assets as we've been explaining throughout this book, beginning at the bottom of the YOU, Inc. Hierarchy and working your way upward.

The interesting paradox is this: when it comes to *earning* your wealth, a narrow focus is the key. But when it comes to *keeping* your wealth, a wide diversification is necessary. Narrow to earn, wide to keep. This chapter will teach you how to properly diversify your assets to allow you to weather any storm and preserve your wealth over the long haul.

> The interesting paradox is this: when it comes to *earning* your wealth, a narrow focus is the key. But when it comes to *keeping* your wealth, a wide diversification is necessary.

Modern (or Markowitz) Portfolio Theory (MPT)

Back in chapter 4, we learned that the efficient market hypothesis (EMH) is a theory claiming that all relevant information about a security is already contained in its price. Ultimately, there are so many investors and information is so abundant that there is no "inefficiency" in the market. If there are any deals lying around, they won't last but for an instant and then will be gone. Those who adhere to this theory say it is futile to try to predict the direction markets will move, and especially to time those movements, and that doing so is no more likely than predicting the next step of a drunken vagrant down the sidewalk. Professor Eugene Fama at the University of Chicago referred to this condition as a "random walk": something totally unpredictable and therefore futile. Later, Princeton professor Burton Malkiel would canonize this illustration in his classic best-selling book *A Random Walk Down Wall Street*.

In 1946 a graduate student at the University of Chicago named Harry Markowitz wrote his doctoral dissertation on risk and return. What he discovered was that if an investor owns two different stocks, the risk of owning one is balanced out a little by the risk of owning another. If an investor owned enough different stocks in his portfolio, the individual risks would cancel one another out, leaving only something called *market risk*.

The idea is this: nobody can really beat the market, and attempting to do so is a fool's game. The best that can be done is to buy into the entire market and ride it upward, as over time, the markets have a tremendous upward bias. The only risk being taken on, in that case, is the risk of the overall market itself. For his (and others') work, Markowitz and his colleagues won the Nobel Prize in 1990, and the individual investor got something called the *Modern* (or *Markowitz*) *Portfolio Theory* (MPT).

MPT says that diversifying the assets you own has the tendency to mitigate risk. As Russell Wild wrote, "What the theory says is that the volatility/risk of a portfolio may differ dramatically from the volatility/risk of the portfolio's components. In other words, you can have two assets with both high standard deviations and high potential returns, but when combined they give you a portfolio with modest standard deviation but the same high potential return."

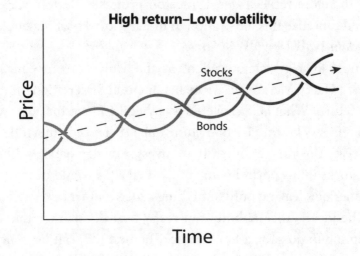

High return–Low volatility

Price

Stocks

Bonds

Time

Did you catch that? You can have individual securities with high volatility, but if you blend enough of them together, your overall portfolio will be less volatile yet still carry the potential for upward growth. It sounds almost too good to be true, except that it has been tested now for more than half a century and has continued to prove itself over and over. Even those who don't entirely believe in the efficient market hypothesis and the resulting Modern Portfolio Theory still believe in the primary tactic that resulted from them: namely, *diversification*.

As we've stated, owning several stocks seems to cancel out the risk of any of the individual ones. But you would still have the movement of all of those stocks, or the entire stock market, as your risk factor. But what if you also bought into a nice variety of bonds? Bonds as an asset class do not *correlate* in their price movement very well with stocks, meaning that sometimes the price of stocks goes up while bonds go down, sometimes it's the opposite, and sometimes they move together. Because of this lack of correlation between these two distinct asset classes, owning a collection of each tends to cancel out the other collection's risk. By *diversifying* your holdings into both bonds and stocks, you smooth out the volatility of your portfolio but still capture the upward potential of both asset classes.

What if you added a third asset class, such as commodities? Then you would have even better diversification, less correlation among your holdings, and less overall portfolio risk. Get the idea? It becomes readily apparent why diversification is such a buzzword in investing today—because it works.

Recall the concept with which we opened the chapter, that in order to *make* your money you need to focus and concentrate your forces. In order to *preserve* your money, you need to distribute your forces and diversify. It's a little like being careful not to risk too much of your army all at once or in one place. After all, that's really what cost Napoleon at Waterloo and Pickett at Gettysburg. By spreading out your wealth and diversifying it across many different asset classes, you have prevented the possibility of too many of your soldiers getting wiped out at one time.

Diversification

You've done a good job if you've stayed with us this long, wading through a lot of information about many different entities. Remember the huge list of assets we covered on the left side of the Risk Meter in chapter 6, and then the "shortcut" vehicles for buying into those assets in chapter 7? This is where it all comes together and we get to start having some fun with all that you've learned. Diversifying is a lot like playing with a set of Lego building bricks; you get to take individual pieces and make them into something cool.

We already touched on the first consideration when putting together a diversified portfolio: *correlation*. A properly diversified portfolio contains assets from classes that do not correlate closely with each other in their market price movements. We mentioned bonds and stocks, which are the two biggies, and also commodities. But there are also real estate, precious metals, and a host of other slices into which you can divide your portfolio which have little or no correlation with each other. This is important.

You also want to diversify *within* those asset classes. For instance, you don't want to own only one or two *types* of stock. In stock investing, there are a couple of different ways to think about diversifying. One popular way to do so is with the following "style grid."

	Value Stocks	Mid-Priced Stocks	Growth Stocks	
				Big Companies
				Mid-Sized Companies
				Small Companies

This grid shows the combinations of the different stock styles with which you can diversify your holdings. On the left are the affordable *value* stocks, and on the right are the expensive *growth* stocks. In between are stocks called *blend*. Value stocks generally pay nice dividends and have low price-to-earnings (P/E) ratios but cannot usually be expected to rise much in price. Growth stocks are just the opposite, while, of course, blend stocks are in between.

On the right side of the grid you can see at the top *large cap* companies (which we defined in chapter 6). At the bottom right are *small cap* companies, and in between are the *mid caps*. One way to diversify your stock holdings is to make sure you have a nice combination of stocks from each of the nine boxes on this grid.

There is another approach to stock diversification, which involves buying stocks across different *sectors*. We also defined sectors in chapter 6, and you'll remember that they included energy, financials, health care, consumer staples, etc. This method works too, but most experts prefer the style method above.

There are also different styles of bonds, including a combination of the many types we discussed in chapter 6. Another factor to consider is domestic and foreign, for both stocks and bonds. In essence, proper diversification combines different asset classes of different styles from different regions of the world, and even those traded in differing currencies. The list below may be a handy guide to keep in mind when seeking to maximize your diversification:

1. stocks
   a. large-cap
   b. mid-cap
   c. small-cap
   d. growth
   e. value
   f. domestic
   g. international
      i. mature market
      ii. emerging market
      iii. frontier

2. bonds
    a. short-term
    b. intermediate-term
    c. long-term
    d. corporate
        i. investment grade
        ii. junk
    e. inflation protected
    f. municipal
    g. foreign sovereign
    h. foreign corporate
3. commodities
4. precious metals
5. real estate (through REITs)

Obviously there are more assets, as we learned when working our way up the Risk Meter. In addition to what is listed above, you should have your emergency savings account, cash on hand, physical gold and silver bullion, life insurance and annuities all in place. Then, for the purpose of this discussion, we'll confine ourselves to the above categories. This is because each of these is easily represented by purchases you can make buy buying ETFs through a brokerage firm. Simply open an account with one of the biggest and best-known names (such as TD Ameritrade, E Trade, Scott Trade, Fidelity, Vanguard, etc.), and once you begin transferring money into that account, you can then begin buying ETFs for each of the above asset classes. One reminder: always manage your costs very closely. Choose a brokerage firm that offers commission-free ETF trades (as do most of the ones we listed above) and very low commissions otherwise. A second reminder: remember to choose low operating expense index ETFs for each of the asset classes in which you choose to invest.

Asset Allocation

So much for diversification; now it's time to consider *how much* to put into each of the diverse assets you've chosen. This is a critical part of building your portfolio and usually goes by the term *asset allocation*. It means what portion of your money you will invest in each of the asset categories discussed above. This is very important. Burton Malkiel wrote, "90 percent of an investor's total return is determined by the asset categories that are selected and their overall proportional representation."

There are (as by now you are not surprised to learn) many different theories as to how to properly allocate your assets. Some people adhere to some cute rules such as subtracting your age from the number 100. The resulting number is the percentage of your portfolio you should invest in stocks (with the assumption being that the remaining percentage would then be invested in bonds). The idea is that the younger you are, the more risky a portfolio you can tolerate because you've got longer to live and therefore outgrow any volatility or downturns in your stock values. Since stocks are considered more risky than bonds, a portfolio for either a younger person, or a person with a high tolerance for risk, should therefore contain more stocks. This is one way to go about it, and is usually referred to as a *life cycle guide* to allocation.

Another way is to consult the experts, who have proven track records of helping others establish proper allocations. For instance, Burton Malkiel recommends the following:

Age: Mid-Twenties
    Cash = 5%
    Bonds = 15%
    Stocks = 70%
    Real Estate = 10%

Age: Late Thirties to Early Forties
    Cash = 5%
    Bonds = 20%
    Stocks = 65%
    Real Estate = 10%

Age: Mid-Fifties
    Cash = 5%
    Bonds = 27.5%
    Stocks = 55%
    Real Estate = 12.5%

Age: Late Sixties and Beyond
    Cash = 10%
    Bonds = 35%
    Stocks = 40%
    Real Estate = 15%

Legendary value investor Benjamin Graham wrote about asset allocation, "We have suggested a fundamental guiding rule that the investor should never have less than 25% or more than 75% of his funds in common stocks, with a consequent inverse range of between 75% and 25% in bonds."

Finally, we offer you the allocation advice of the manager of the world's largest hedge fund, Ray Dalio of Bridgewater Associates. Dalio recommends the following:

Long-Term US Bonds = 40%
Intermediate US Bonds = 15%
Stocks = 30%
Commodities = 7.5%
Gold = 7.5%

So there you have it: even the experts don't agree! But notice that each of these follows the same general principles of diversification, and the truth is, if you choose one of these recommended allocations, or something close, and fill them out with diversified selections of individual assets through low cost index ETFs, you will probably do quite well over time. Again, analyze your particular situation, taking into account your age, plans for retirement, and risk tolerance, and then select an asset allocation plan that is right for you.

Do It Yourself or Trust It to Someone Else?

One question about all of this is whether you should try "doing it yourself." In other words, do you have what it takes to open up a brokerage account, shop for the different index ETFs representing various asset classes, and put together your own portfolio? At first it may seem confusing, complicated, and overwhelming. The purpose of this book is to show you that while this can get complicated and overblown, it doesn't have to be that way, especially with a little education.

For instance, now you have at least some familiarity with the different asset classes and the general concept of diversifying yourself across those classes, and you can pick the expert's advice you feel fits your particular situation regarding asset allocation. All that's left is to do a little shopping. Trust us, it can be fun, and you can do it.

But wait a moment! If you really want to simplify things, there are ETFs that represent the entire bond market! That's right, they hold in proportion pretty much all the major bond offerings in the whole bond market. Buy that one ETF, and you've got your bond allocation covered! There are similar ETFs for the stock markets. By selecting one or two of these and then buying them in the percentages recommended by the experts above, you're done! Just keep investing that same amount each month with your dollar cost averaging amount, and you've got it. Over time, especially over the long haul, you will be shocked at how well you do as a do-it-yourselfer compared to the experts.

On the other hand, this may feel like too much for you to handle. Or you may have enough money that you don't care if you spend another 1 or 2 percent per year to get a professional to do basically what we just showed you how to do for free. And don't get us wrong, there are some very competent advisers out there who are worth the money—especially those who work as fiduciaries and are not paid based upon what they get you to invest in but rather just collect a fee from you for their time. John Bogle wrote, "I endorse the idea that for many . . . investors, financial advisers may provide a valuable service in giving you peace of mind, in helping you establish a sensible fund portfolio that matches your appetite for reward and your tolerance for risk, and in helping you stay the course in troubled waters. But the evidence . . . confirms my original hypothesis that, vital as those services may be, advisers as a group cannot be credibly relied on to add value by selecting winning funds for you."

Ultimately, the choice will be up to you. But no matter which route you select, remember what we told you earlier: always keep an eye on your own money, and never let it get too far out of your sight. No one will ever care about it as much as you.

NINE

Putting It All Together

*"There are two times in a man's life when he should not
speculate: when he can't afford it, and when he can."*
—MARK TWAIN

Let's review where we are. First of all, you're going to utilize the
many tools from the defense of personal finance that we taught
in the *Financial Fitness* book and eliminate your consumer debt
(and stay out of it for the rest of your life)! Next you are going to
establish your emergency savings account, do some basic survival preparation, and all the while funnel as much money as you
can into yourself and your primary method of earning money.
By doing this latter part, you are feeding the goose that lays the
proverbial golden eggs and playing offense. Perhaps this is a business or a career, but you realize that maximizing the investment
in yourself is the best investment you will ever make.

Then, with any excess money beyond that you will begin investing in the various assets listed on the left side of the Risk
Meter, in general working from the bottom up. This includes getting your tax and legal advisers in place, getting your will and
powers of attorney prepared, and making sure you and your
family are properly insured in all the necessary areas. Further,
you have selected the asset allocation plan that suits you best and
will begin buying index ETFs in proportion to that allocation
in a brokerage account you will open yourself or through a full
service provider you will pay to do it for you. You will also max

out any contributions into the tax-advantaged accounts such as 401(k)s and IRAs for which you are eligible (and will consider these when looking at your overall asset allocation). Then, on a monthly basis you will continue to buy into your portfolio of assets in the exact proportion you have determined through the process of dollar cost averaging. Finally, you will do all of this for the long term.

What could go wrong?

Speculation

Burton Malkiel wrote, "It is not hard, really, to make money in the market . . . . [A]n investor who simply buys and holds a broad-based portfolio of stocks can make reasonably generous long-run returns. What is hard to avoid is the alluring temptation to throw your money away on short, get-rich-quick speculative binges," and reaching the poetic heights, he wrote, "The psychology of speculation is a veritable theater of the absurd."

> "The psychology of speculation is a veritable theater of the absurd."
> —Burton Malkiel

For some reason when people get interested in investing, they have a tendency to go off track by thinking they can beat the market. They are just sure some stock they heard about on television or from a friend is going to take off and make them a lot of money! They get enthusiastic about investing and wind up speculating instead. As Benjamin Graham wrote, "While enthusiasm may be necessary for great accomplishments elsewhere, on Wall Street it almost invariably leads to disaster. For indeed, the investor's chief problem—and even his worst enemy—is likely to be himself." Jason Zweig wrote, "Once you lose 95% of your money, you have to gain 1,900% *just to get back to where you started*. Taking a foolish risk can put you so deep in the hole that it's virtually impossible to get out" (emphasis his).

Don't think you are above being tempted to speculate. Some of the greatest minds in history have ignored logic and jumped in with emotion. Sir Isaac Newton, whom we have to thank for his laws of physics, got caught up in the wild speculation of the South Sea Company bubble in his day and lost a fortune. Mark Twain, quoted at the top of this chapter, couldn't help himself and continued throughout his life to lose spectacular sums of money on wild investments. To quote Jason Zweig once more, "Never fool yourself into confusing speculation with investment."

Unless you are going to be a professional who pursues finances as a full-time occupation, investing is supposed to be a sideline venture. It is intended to preserve and amplify the fruits of your labor that result from doing what you do. Make sure the main thing continues to be the main thing, and keep your focus on the goose that lays the golden eggs. Then set up your investments to be done on an automatic and long-term basis as we've taught in this book, and keep away from it. Just let it grow unmolested.

Start Now

Malkiel wrote, "The single most important thing you can do to achieve financial security is to begin a regular savings program and to start it as early as possible. It is critically important to start saving now. Trust in time rather than timing."

It may be too late to start saving and investing those savings from a young age. Or maybe you

> **"Trust in time rather than timing."**
> —**Burton Malkiel**

are young and this is your chance not to blow it! Either way, you can only start when you can start, and that time should be now, no matter your age! Don't forget the power of compound interest over time and the value of putting it to work for you.

Author Jeremy Siegel calculated the returns from various asset classes from the year 1800 through 2014. A single dollar invested in stocks in 1802 would have grown to a staggering $18 million by 2013! If you look at the chart below, from a thirty-thousand-foot view, you can easily see that asset classes tend to move steadily upward over time. The idea is to get on board and ride it upward yourself. This can only be done with a long-term view, one that doesn't worry about the day-to-day fluctuations and hysterias that pervade our modern investing world. Just know that time is your friend, and play it accordingly.

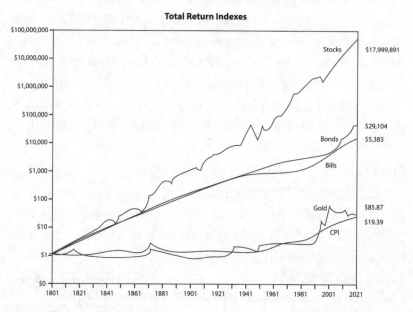

Burton Malkiel – *Total Return Indexes*

Malkiel wrote, "You can only get poor quickly. To get rich, you will have to do it slowly, and you have to start now." While you may be able to get rich fairly quickly in your primary career or through the business you are building (especially if your name is Mark Zuckerberg), when it comes to investing and preserving the fruits of your labor, Malkiel is absolutely correct; *it takes time!* Get started now, and put the power of compounding to work for you.

Maximize What You Invest

Just as it is important to start as soon as possible putting the power of compounding to work for you, you should also go in as big as you can. Consider the table below demonstrating the difference between investing $20 a month at 9 percent compound interest vs. $100 a month at the same rate.

Year	$20 monthly	$100 monthly
10	$3,900	$19,500
20	$13,460	$67,300
30	$36,890	$184,450
40	$94,330	$471,650

The difference at the forty-year mark is a staggering $377,320, just because you managed to find another $80 to sock away each month!

So think about where you can cut back or scrimp. A little here and a little there can add up to huge differences over time.

Manage Your Costs

We've hit this before, but we feel the need to hit it again. Manage the ongoing costs of your investments with ferocity. Just a percentage or two over time can make a huge difference in the accumulation of wealth. As we saw in the table above, in which a larger regular amount invested built up to an enormously bigger sum over time, the same goes with your net rate of return. Your *net rate of return* is your actual percentage gain after paying expenses (payments to your adviser and the managers of your ETFs, commissions on trades, etc.).

To illustrate just how powerful a slight difference in the rate of return can be, consider the "rule of 72." You may be familiar with this handy rule of thumb. It basically states that the number of years required for your money to double can be found quickly by taking the real rate of return and dividing it into the number 72. For instance, if you are receiving approximately a 7 percent annual compounded return, it would take about ten years for your money to double (7 into 72 goes about 10 times). But if you could boost that percentage by just a few, say to 10 percent, you would now be doubling your money in closer to seven years!

So the net percent return you get on your investments is very important when considering the power of compounding over time. Fight for every last little percentage you can with your investments, and don't waste any of it.

Rebalance Your Allocations

The important considerations of asset allocation we covered in the last chapter are funny in one way: they change over time. No, we don't mean the fact that if you are following the life cycle strategy for asset allocation, you will want to change the amount of money you put into stocks versus bonds as you hit a different season in life. That may be true. What we mean is that the various assets in your portfolio will grow at different rates over time. The result is that your carefully planned-out asset allocation percentages will drift away from your original intent.

Let's say you decided upon Ray Dalio's recommendation of 40 percent long-term US bonds, 15 percent intermediate term US bonds, 30 percent stocks, 7.5 percent commodities, and 7.5 percent gold. You set yourself up with index ETFs representing these classes (with the exception of the gold, which you may have chosen to buy in physical bullion), and put your money into them every month in these proportions. But in your first year stocks really take off, while bonds take a dip. Commodities and gold grow nicely. At the end of that first year your asset allocation might end up looking like the following:

Long-Term US Bonds = 36.5% (down 3.5%)
Intermediate US Bonds = 13.5% (down 1.5%)
Stocks = 35% (up 5%)
Commodities = 7.5% (steady)
Gold = 7.5% (steady)

In this case you can see that your original intent for these proportions is no longer in place. Why does this matter? At first, especially after just one year, it may not matter all that much. But again, over time, the situation could drift far from your original intent, resulting in a much riskier portfolio than you originally designed or a much more conservative one. It could also mean that when stocks start to nose-dive a few years from now and bonds take off, you have too many stocks and not enough bonds, and you lose out on both ends much worse than you would have if you'd stayed aligned to the percentages Dalio recommended.

For this reason it is important to periodically do something called *rebalancing*. This simply means to sell off the excess and reinvest it in the categories that are lagging. Most experts recommend doing this at least once a year, but some say to do it as often as every six months. You want to be careful doing it too often, however, because buying and selling will likely incur some commissions, and you remember what we said about keeping those expenses low.

The other reason this is a good idea is because it allows you to cash out a little bit on the assets that have appreciated in price, "taking some of your winnings," so to speak, and then reinvest them in those asset classes that are depressed. This effectively locks in some of your gains while forcing you to buy other assets when they are cheap.

By the way, this is almost exactly contrary to what the average investor does. She gets caught up in emotional moves of the market, chases the hottest property, and almost always ends up selling low and buying high, even though she really wants to do the opposite. It is one thing to know logically that you should buy when things are cheap. It is another thing to be able to do so when everybody is jumping out of a particular investment because it "went down." Once something has "gone down" is the exact time it has gone "on sale," but it doesn't feel this way to the speculator because he is following every swing and sway of the market.

Rebalancing your portfolio at least once a year takes this good idea (buying low and selling high), which you probably agree with logically, and mechanizes it so you will actually do it. Remember, the secret to investing the way these experts teach is to do all of this dispassionately and mechanically, ignoring the chatter and noise coming from the markets. Rebalancing will automatically, unemotionally, consistently, and periodically lock in your winnings and force you to buy other assets while they are on sale.

Write Yourself an Investment Contract

You may be getting the idea that investing is not that difficult if you can put it all on autopilot and keep your hands off the controls. To be quite honest, this is one of the advantages of simply hiring a fiduciary money manager to do it all for you, although this brings the two disadvantages of expense and the tendency for you to not watch your money closely enough. However, if you can set things up in a way that you can allow them to roll on automatically without sabotaging them, then doing this yourself is no big deal.

One interesting approach to this is to sign a contract with yourself. Proposed by Jason Zweig, a personal contract compels you to make a commitment out of your good intentions. It may seem a little hokey, but we've never been stopped by hokey before! Below is a modified version of the original he proposed.

I, _____, hereby state that I am an investor seeking to accumulate wealth for the long term.

I realize there will be times when I am tempted to get caught up in speculation because a particular stock or bond has "gone up" or is a "hot tip" or "sure thing." I may also get panicked like everyone else and be tempted to sell out on good investments merely because they have "gone down."

I hereby declare my refusal to allow a mob or herd of strangers to have input into my financial future. I don't run with mobs or herds anyway.

I also promise myself not to invest simply because the market itself has "gone up" or sell because it has "gone down." Instead, I will be methodical and mature about my investing, killing consumer debt like a cancer, pouring all I can into myself and my primary income source and/or business, consistently using the surplus to accumulate assets over time.

I will invest $_____.00 per month into my education, self, primary income source and/or business.

I will then invest $ _____.00 per month, each and every month, no matter what, through an automatic investment plan or Dollar Cost Averaging program, into the following overall asset allocation:

_____ %

_____%
_____%
_____%
_____%
_____%
_____%

I will also invest additional amounts whenever I can.

I hereby declare that I will hold each of these investments continually until at least the following date (a minimum of 10 years from the date of this contract): _____, 20_____. (I will allow exceptions to this for an emergency over which I otherwise would have no control, such as a major accident, loss of primary income, or something equally devastating.)

By signing below, I am stating to myself my intention to abide by these terms and to reread this document each month when I am reviewing my dollar cost averaging purchases or whenever I am tempted to follow the herd and sell or buy merely because of mob sentiment.

This contract is valid only once signed by me (and spouse, if jointly declared) and by at least one witness.

Signed (spouse #1)   Date:

_____   _____

Signed (spouse #2)

_____   _____

Witness

_____   _____

The Future

When taking responsibility for your finances and getting your investment life straight, it is customary to consider the future. After all, everything we've discussed in this book is geared toward doing things properly so that in the future your assets will grow and bring you back more assets. Investing, by its very nature, is a "future thing."

The danger is to become too much of a prognosticator of the future, peering too hard around the corners of tomorrow and trying to decipher how things will shake out. Some people who do so turn into Chicken Littles and run around crying: "The sky is falling, the sky is falling!" They see a total collapse of the monetary system and blood in the streets. Others get optimistic and think a particular asset class is going to take off to the moon, and they become overly exuberant to the point of irrationality. The truth is, as John Bogle's friend told him years ago, "Nobody knows nothin.'"

One of the reasons to take Bogle's advice and stay completely away from the daily chatter coming out of Wall Street and the daily financial news outlets is because if you properly construct your investment strategy as we've taught in these pages (as proven by many experts over many years), you will have done the best you can to weather any storm and ride any trend. Let's take a look at some very possible future scenarios and see how the investment policies advanced in this book would serve you.

When it gets right down to it, there are really only four things that can happen in the future. The first one is that everything will stay exactly the same as it is today and nothing will change at all. You know that isn't going to happen, so we can just eliminate that one right off the bat and say that there are only three possibilities. And through each of these situations, know that the risk factors we discussed in chapter 5 are hard at work, acting like a headwind to stop you and your investments from making progress. It is best never to forget that the Financial Matrix is real.

Inflation

First, we could end up in a situation in which we have inflation. If you'll remember, inflation occurs when the money supply expands to such a point that it drives the prices of everything *up* and therefore the value (or purchasing power) of the dollar *down*. In a condition of inflation, gold has been a great hedge. This is because as the paper currency loses its value, gold stands there like the standard that it is and holds its own value. Stocks also seem to do well in inflationary periods, as long as they belong to companies that can raise prices as inflation eats away at buying power.

Real estate also does well during inflation, because a good home on decent property has a value to the homeowner all its own, no matter what is happening in the world of money. But real estate does one other thing during times of increasing inflation. Malkiel writes that "real estate returns seem to be higher than stock returns during periods when inflation is accelerating.

. . . [R]eal estate has proved to be a good investment providing generous returns and excellent inflation-hedging characteristics." This is partly because the real estate market is less efficient than the stock and bond markets, prices move more slowly and more invisibly, and people get emotional about buying homes, *and* finally, everybody needs a place to live.

Also, securities such as TIPS (Treasury Inflation Protected Securities) do well too, because the interest rate goes up to compensate for the rate of inflation. Additionally, having cash flow from a profitable business of your own is a great hedge against inflation, as the prices a business charges can generally be raised to compensate for the decline in purchasing power.

A subcondition would be one of *hyperinflation*. This is the condition in which inflation runs out of control and advances quickly. This has led to the destruction of currencies and is a catastrophic financial occurrence. Again, "hard" assets like gold, real property, and customers from a business (who will have to pay in *some* kind of tender) are the best hedges in such cases.

Deflation

Deflation is the condition in which money gains in value because the amount in circulation is becoming more and more scarce. This can happen when investors and buyers are rattled by a shrinking economy, and people are afraid to buy or invest in new economic growth. This is effectively what happened during the Great Depression. There was money, but it went into hiding. Prices can come down *some*, which is good for consumers, but the lack of income caused panic.

During times of deflation, any type of investment that has a guaranteed rate of return such as bonds, cash value life insurance policies, and annuities do very well. This is because you are promised a certain return, and the money you've been promised in dollar terms is getting more and more valuable (grows in its buying power). It is also good to have cash during deflation, as that is what becomes scarce and what everybody wants and needs. And for sure, having positive cash flow from a profitable business selling things people need is one of the greatest protections.

Gold, too, is a good hedge even for deflation because the prices of goods other than gold will go down faster than the dollar price of gold. To quote James Rickards, "If gold is going down in nominal terms, yet other prices are going down more, gold will still preserve wealth when measured in real terms." Further, many governments are already experimenting with *negative* interest rates in order to combat deflation, meaning you will actually be *charged* to deposit your money in a bank! Under such absurd conditions, the cost of storing a little gold suddenly doesn't seem like such an inconvenience.

Stagnation

Not to be confused with *stagflation*, which is a term coined to represent a slowing economy in which both the unemployment rate and inflation rates are high (another proof of the fallacy of that terrible Phillips curve!), stagnation is basically what Japan's economy has been experiencing for more than twenty years. Stagnation is a general movement sideways in the markets, with no real growth or expansion of the economy. Under this condition, it is hard to make money investing because nothing really goes up or down by any appreciable amount.

Again, the best hedges here are assets with real value and a healthy ongoing cash flow from a profitable business. Hard assets are particularly valuable here, but stocks and bonds and many of the other paper instruments will prove frustratingly benign.

Perhaps a little analogy will be useful. These three conditions, inflation, deflation, and stagnation, can be analogized with water. If money were water, inflation would be the condition wherein water is abundant, but it is increasingly less useful as water. How could this occur? Think of salt water in the ocean. One can die of thirst surrounded by endless waves. So inflation is the condition in which water becomes more and more salty.

If money were water, deflation would be the condition wherein water becomes more and more scarce. In other words, deflation is a drought. Imagine your well going dry and cisterns drying up. As water disappears, people panic. This is precisely what occurs with money during deflation.

Finally, if money were water, stagnation is a stagnant pond. There is water there, but it is motionless and increasingly slack. There are no springs of freshwater feeding into it. It just sits there without being replenished, deteriorating because there is no regenerative source flowing into it.

Notice that in all three of these conditions, our properly diversified portfolio has given us some protection. Notice too the importance of positive cash flow from our assets, but also, if possible, from a business over which we have control. In the water analogy, positive cash flow is like a freshwater spring: it is the solution to all three conditions! Therefore, our smartest move today to prepare for the uncertainty of tomorrow is to use our energies to develop cash flow from assets and businesses.

Notice also the importance of preserving some value in an investment like gold, which sits on the sidelines untouched by central bank machinations. In addition to having positive cash flows from assets and businesses, it is wise to preserve some of our capital in tamperproof stores of value like precious metals.

No one can know what the future holds. But it is likely that we will see periods described by each of these conditions, likely swinging from one to the other. Those who sufficiently and properly accumulate cash flow–producing assets, we think, will find that they weather any coming storms quite nicely. Sure, there could be some crazy calamitous times ahead. There is always going to be some development that was unforeseen. Nobody knows for sure what tomorrow will bring. But an apocalypse isn't likely. What *is* likely are repeated cycles of the same three conditions in old ways but also in new, unpredicted combinations. The properly diversified, asset-rich, cash-flowed investor will not only survive such times but be in a position to thrive!

Remember What Money Is Really For

We began our journey of going *beyond financial fitness* by describing what money is actually for and how most people have got it wrong. Most think that money is merely there to allow them to buy stuff. If they want more stuff, they need more money. Hopefully by this point, you've now gotten it right! You know confidently that money is to be used to fulfill your life's purpose, buy some security, give to good causes, and serve and protect those you love and the causes you care about.

You now know that the way to handle money is to always be giving a generous portion away, while paying yourself first for your savings and investments. You have learned that the wealthy understand that every dollar they earn today represents a possible ten dollars down the road, if only they will invest that dollar into interest-compounding assets. Further, you've learned that your best asset is yourself, and the best investment you can ever make is in what you do to earn your income, whether your career or your business. The big lesson, though, is that money should be used throughout your life to accumulate assets that also bring you more money.

There is a warning to be given here, however. When reading through the abundance of literature available on investing and accumulating assets, one can easily get the idea that the over-arching goal of such endeavors is to set things up so that one can live in comfort at some rosy time in the future. Many books and courses encourage this view. The basic idea seems to be that it is a worthy goal to maximize your own relaxation, comfort, wants, and desires.

There is nothing wrong with this within certain limits, of course. You should be thinking about taking care of yourself financially in the days when your health may no longer allow you to earn a proper living. You should be interested in establishing ongoing cash flow from assets so that you are not required to labor at something for which your heart doesn't yearn. And you should be considering the inheritance you'll leave and the legacy you'll establish. After all, the Bible says, "a good man leaves an inheritance to his children's children."

But if you exert yourself to do all this investing merely to set yourself up for a selfish, hedonistic, materialistic utopian *some-day*, you will be miserable. The reason is because we are not wired to be happy when we seek to directly make ourselves so. In the explicit pursuit of pleasure, we end up with emptiness and boredom (not to mention a wasted life). Only in pursuing something larger than ourselves, causes that don't have anything to do with our selfish little desires, and in helping others, do we truly find fulfillment. As we have written elsewhere, the only way to *be* happy is to *give* happy.

Therefore, go ahead and learn all this investing knowledge. Apply it and prosper. Accumulate assets like a Rockefeller if you want to, but be careful where your heart is during the whole endeavor. It is okay to *have money*, but it is not okay for money to *have you*. Be sure your main focus is on what money can do in service to your higher calling, and not just in service to your highest wants. May you make the biggest difference in the world that you can, as long as you can, and for as many as you can. We wish you all the prosperity you (and the power of compounding) are willing to earn!

Onward

It is only fitting to close out our study with two of the icons of the investing world. Benjamin Graham wrote, "The real money in investment will have to be made—as most of it has been made in the past—*not out of buying and selling but of owning and holding securities*, receiving interest and dividends and increases in value" (emphasis his). And in the words of Warren Buffett, "By periodically investing in an index fund, the know-nothing investor can actually out-perform most investment professionals. Paradoxically, when 'dumb' money acknowledges its limitations, it ceases to be dumb."

401(k)s: Tax-advantaged savings accounts in the United States into which pretax dollars (up to a limit) can be contributed by qualified participants (those beneath certain income limits). The money inside these accounts can then be invested in a number of vehicles, and the growth occurs tax-free. At age 59½ withdrawals can be made without penalty (although the gains at that time will be taxed). At age 70½ there are required minimum distributions that must be taken out.

403(b)s, 457(b)s: Tax-advantaged savings accounts for those employed by tax-exempt and government organizations, respectively. (see **401(k)s**)

529 Savings Accounts: In the United States, tax-advantaged savings accounts to be used exclusively for educational purposes.

Active vs. Passive Income: Active income is earned as a result of work you do, so it requires your active participation to get it; passive income keeps paying you even if you stop working.

Angel Investing: Generally the earliest round of equity investing by outsiders toward the starting of a business. Sometimes this is seed capital, but it could also come after the founders have put in their own seed capital. Angel investors are usually wealthy individuals or groups seeking to get in early in a good startup opportunity.

Animal Spirits: The unpredictable and sometimes inexplicable behavior of investors in public financial markets.

Annuity: A financial contract in which an amount of money is paid in (either all at once or over time) and then, upon initiation at some point in the future, ongoing payouts are made to the bearer. Annuities with something called a lifetime income rider are one of the only ways to make sure you don't outlive your money. There are, in general, three main types of annuities: variable, fixed, and indexed (or hybrid indexed).

Ask: The lowest price a prospective seller is willing to accept for a good. (see **Bid**)

Asset: Something owned that has value because it either brings positive cash flow to its owner or has the potential to do so in the future.

Asset Allocation Plan: Details how much money you will keep in different investment categories.

Asset Class: A category of assets, such as stocks, bonds, commodities, precious metals, real estate, and the like.

Assets vs. Liabilities: An asset is something you own that brings you additional money while a liability is something that owns you because it costs you additional money.

Beneficiary: The person or entity you designate to receive your life insurance death benefit upon your passing (also may be used to describe the recipient of any other assets from your estate).

Bid: The highest price a buyer is willing to pay for a good. (see **Ask**)

Bonds: A financial vehicle that basically represents an IOU. Bonds are issued for a face amount (meaning the amount of money that will be returned at the end of the loan period, which is called the date of maturity). The interest paid (usually twice per year) is called the coupon rate. Bonds can be bought and sold on the open market.

Brokerage House (or Broker): A financial company/person active as a custodian of your paper investments usually offering a range of services including savings interest, stock and bond trading, etc.

Bullion: A precious metal that has not been manufactured into a sovereign coin. Bullion may be in the form of rounds, bars, or other shapes and types that are not denominated by a government as money.

Callable Bond: A bond that can be redeemed by the issuer prior to its maturity. For instance, if interest rates have declined since the company first issued the bond, the company may decide to refinance its debt at the new lower rate of interest. It would do this by "calling" the current outstanding bonds by paying them off early, then issuing new bonds for which it would have to pay only the new, lower interest rate.

Capital Gain: The increase in price of an asset. For instance, if a share of Ford Motor Company increased from $12 to $13, the shareholder would have experienced a $1 capital gain. In the United States, for tax purposes, there are two types of capital gains: short term and long term. Short-term capital gains are taxed at a higher rate and apply to gains realized in one year and one day, or less. Long-term capital gains are taxed at a lower rate and are for gains realized on an asset during a period longer than one year and one day. (see **Realized Capital Gain**)

Certificates of Deposit (CDs): A savings vehicle in which one deposits money for a predetermined period of time at an agreed interest rate. Early withdrawal carries stiff penalties, but the interest rates are usually better than regular savings accounts.

Commodity: A raw material or primary product that can be bought and sold.

Compound Interest: Interest paid on both the principal and the accrued interest. You are charged interest on something you financed, and then on a later day, you are also charged interest on the earlier interest. People who pay compound interest usually end up spending much more money than their purchases are worth, while those who collect it make money faster than others.

Comprehensive Financial Plan: outlines how you will earn, save, spend, borrow, and invest your money.

Creditors: People or entities to which a person or business owes money.

Cyclical Stock: A stock from a corporation that sells products that are not *needs* for consumers, but rather *wants*. (see **Defensive Stock**)

Debt: Money owed to someone or some entity. Most debt should be avoided, especially consumer debt.

Default: Failure to meet the legal requirements of a loan or financial arrangement. The money is owed, but it does not get repaid.

Defensive Stock: Not to be confused with defense stocks, which are those of companies who supply the military, defensive stocks are those from companies that make products consumers must have all the time just to live. (see **cyclical stock**)

Deflation: The opposite of inflation, deflation is the increase in the spending power of money due to a lower and lower amount of it in circulation.

Delayed Gratification: The state of waiting to spend money on things until you can truly afford them.

Depreciation: The decrease in value of an asset over time. Never use credit to finance something that depreciates.

Diversification: The strategy of mixing up your assets so you are not overexposed to any one category. This helps protect your portfolio from too much volatility in one area.

Dividends: The (usually) quarterly sharing of corporate earnings paid out to shareholders of a stock.

Dollar Cost Averaging: A strategy wherein an investor places a fixed amount into a given investment on a regular basis. This is intended to occur every month regardless of what is occurring in the financial markets.

Durable Power of Attorney: This document takes over if you are incapacitated and unable to make decisions on your own. It specifies a person you name who will be legally designated to take care of two primary things: your finances and your health care decisions (these can be two different people, if you so desire).

Efficient Market Hypothesis (EMH): A theory claiming that all the relevant investment information is already contained in the price of an asset. The idea is that there is so much abundant information immediately available to everyone that any "deals" in the modern markets would be snatched up before anyone could find out about it. While most believe that this theory is not strictly true, it does serve as a valid warning against mere amateurs attempting to "beat the market."

Emergency Fund: A fund that covers unexpected or emergency expenses when they come. Those who are financially fit consistently (and often automatically) pay some of their income to this fund with the goal of accumulating at least three to six months' worth of living expenses.

Emerging Market: An economy with a low to middle per capita income. (see **Mature Market** and **Frontier Market**)

Entrepreneur: A person who takes the risk to build things and create increased value and profits. Societies that incentivize entrepreneurial success are more free and prosperous than those that do not.

Equity: One's ownership in an asset once all debts associated with that asset are paid off.

Equities: Stocks or any other security representing an ownership interest in a company.

Exchange-Traded Fund (ETF): A mutual fund that trades like a stock. These are generally index funds and have super low expense ratios. Like mutual funds, they are available in a variety of asset classes.

Fannie Mae: The nickname for the Federal National Mortgage Association (FNMA), a government-sponsored enterprise (GSE) created by the U.S. Congress in 1938 for the purpose of flowing money to mortgage lenders to help support home ownership for low, moderate, and middle-income citizens. (see **Freddie Mac**)

Federal Deposit Insurance Corporation (FDIC): An entity established by the US government for the purpose of insuring individual savings deposits up to $250,000.

Federal Reserve (FED): In the United States, this is a private banking cartel established by the US government and tasked with the management of the money supply through manipulation of interest rates.

Fiduciary: A person responsible for managing the assets of another person. Fee-based Fiduciaries make their money based on a flat fee (perhaps an hourly rate or one-time charge), and not from some percentage of the total amount managed or the return on that investment the fiduciary may achieve.

Financial Fitness: The state of understanding and applying the forty-seven laws of financial success covered in the original *Financial Fitness* book.

Financial Matrix: The name given to the largely invisible complicated web of fractional-reserve banking, Federal Reserve banking, and other financial instrumentation that makes it difficult for average people to "make it out alive" financially. The concept is inspired by the major motion picture, *The Matrix*.

Fraud: A financial crime in which deliberate action is taken for financial gain at the expense of someone else.

Freddie Mac: The nickname for the Federal Home Loan Mortgage Corporation (FHLMC), a government-sponsored enterprise (GSE) created by the U.S. Congress in 1970 for the purpose of flowing money to mortgage lenders to help support home ownership for middle-income citizens.
(See **Fannie Mae**)

Frontier Market: A developing country too small or unstable to be generally considered as an emerging market country. (see **Emerging Market** and **Mature Market**)

Goose That Lays the Golden Eggs: Your business or career that is the source of your financial success. Taking care of the goose means taking actions to ensure that your primary income will continue and even grow.

Growth Stock: A stock from a company that is not paying dividends, may be showing little to no earnings yet, but seems to promise tremendous growth in market share and earnings in the future. These stocks are generally said to be "expensive" (meaning their share price is many times their earnings). (see **Value Stock**)

Health Savings Accounts (HSAs): In the United States, tax-free savings accounts to be used for payment of health care expenses, premiums, office visits, etc.

Hedge Fund: A lightly regulated but restricted-access private investment partnership open only to qualified and/or sophisticated investors. Think of a mutual fund on steroids.

Hyperinflation: An extreme case of inflation in which the money supply expands rapidly and the value of that same money precipitously declines.

Index: A measure of value meant to represent a broader market by tracking the aggregate price of a basket of representative securities. For example, the Dow Jones Industrial Average is an index comprised of the 30 largest US companies traded on the New York Stock Exchange.

Index Fund: A type of mutual fund (or exchange-traded fund) designed to match the makeup of a market index, such as the Dow Jones Industrial Index or the Standard & Poor's 500 Index. This allows passive management and the blind following of the performance of the index, as opposed to active fund management and attempts to beat the market. This allows for low operating expenses and a diversified exposure to the market. (see **Mutual Fund**)

Individual Retirement Account (IRA): A savings program in which pretax contributions are made over time into an account that then grows tax free. At a later date, the money can be taken out and will be taxed at that point, when it is assumed the bearer will be in a lower tax bracket.

Inflation: A decrease in the value of money due to a persistent, substantial rise in the general level of prices caused by an increase in the volume of money in circulation. Government production of fiat money often causes this.

Insolvent: Not having enough money to pay one's bills and debts.

Interest Rate: The amount charged, expressed as a percentage of principal, by a lender to a borrower for the use of money.

Internet Bank: A financial institution that exists only online. By not having physical branch locations, such banks can keep expenses to a minimum and offer generally higher interest rates for savings deposits.

Investing: The intelligent, consistent, informed acquiring of assets over time for the purpose of growing overall asset value and developing increased cash flow.

Investment Policy: Spells out your fundamental approach to investing.

Junk Bonds (also called High-Yield Bonds): Corporate bonds issued by companies that are either small, newer on the market, or seen for some reason to be risky. For this reason a high interest rate must be offered in order to entice investors to buy them, and therefore they are called *high yield* or by the more derogatory and memorable term *junk*.

Long: Being involved in an investment in which you hope for the price of your holding to go up. (see **Short**)

Liquidity: The ease with which you can get your money back out of a particular investment vehicle.

Macroeconomics vs. Microeconomics: Macroeconomics is the field of human action that deals with large-scale factors—interest rates, inflation, national taxes and spending, sectors of the economy, etc.—while microeconomics deals with the actions and economic choices of individuals, small groups, and individual businesses.

Margin: Money that is borrowed for the purpose of purchasing securities (stocks, bonds, options, etc.).

Market Capitalization: The total value of all shares of stock outstanding for a corporation. This number can be determined by multiplying the price of a share of stock by the total number of shares outstanding. From this come the terms Small Cap, Mid Cap, and Large Cap companies.

Mature Market: A mature market may be one that has reached equilibrium in prices and is no longer growing substantially. This term may also refer to a market that has stable laws and political situation, and is therefore considered the safest type in which to invest. (See **Emerging Market** and **Frontier Market**)

Modern (or Markowitz) Portfolio Theory: The theory developed by Harry Markowitz (and others) that advanced the notion that the volatility of one asset can be somewhat cancelled out by mixing it with another asset which has its own specific volatility. The idea is that a basket of volatile assets is not nearly as volatile overall as are any of the assets individually.

Money Market Account (MMA): A deposit account in which your money should earn a slightly higher interest rate than it would in a normal savings account. There are usually minimum investment amounts and limits on the number of transactions you are able to make in a month. The interest rate generally fluctuates daily with the rates in the "money markets."

Municipal Bond: A debt security issued by a state, municipality or county for the purpose of financing its capital expenditures, such as the construction of highways, schools, or other infrastructure.

Mutual Fund: A pool of money from individual investors managed by a professional. This money could be invested in stocks, bonds, commodities, or any combination of asset classes. There are two primary types of mutual funds:
>   **Actively Managed Funds:** these involve active trading in which the fund managers attempt to outperform the larger market as a whole.
>   **Passively Managed Funds (usually called Index Funds):** these involve investing in an index in exact proportion to its components and then leaving the money alone. This type of fund delivers the exact market performance and does not speculate in an attempt to accomplish more.

Option: A contract that gives the buyer the right, but not the obligation, to buy or sell an underlying asset at a specific price on or before a certain date.

Paper Gain: An increase (or decrease) in the market value of an asset that will be converted into actual profit (or loss) only when the asset is sold (at which point it would then be considered a realized gain or loss).

Pay Yourself First: This is the first principle and one of the most important factors of financial fitness. This involves regularly setting money aside before allowing it to go to other uses.

Permanent Life Insurance: A life insurance product that not only provides a death benefit but offers wealth building through the accumulation of a cash value over the years as premiums are paid in. There are three main types of permanent life insurance: whole life, universal life, and indexed universal life. (see **Term Insurance**)

Phillips Curve: The supposed inverse relationship between inflation and unemployment. This theory has been largely disproven.

Portfolio: The total collection of your investment assets.

Price to Earnings Ratio (P/E Ratio): The ratio of a company's share price to its per-share earnings. Also called the *price multiple* or the *earnings multiple*.

Principal and Interest: Principal is the original amount of money lent, while interest is the amount you pay to borrow the money to buy something. Sometimes the interest actually costs more than the principal. In most cases, it is best to avoid obligating oneself to pay interest.

Principle: A universal truth that, if applied correctly, always works.

Random Walk Theory: Advanced by author Burton Malkiel (and others), this theory states that predicting the performance of the stock market is no more possible than predicting the next step of a drunken vagrant staggering along the street.

Real Estate Investment Trust (REIT): A company formed according to specific trust laws that manages a collection of income-producing real estate. Shares of REITs can be bought and sold similarly to mutual funds.

Realized Capital Gain: The increase in the value of an asset "locked in" for tax purposes by the fact that you sold it. You have "realized" that gain by selling it and now owe taxes on the amount the asset has appreciated from the time you purchased it until the time you sold it. (see **Capital Gain**)

Rebalancing: The act of selling some securities and buying others in the correct amounts in order to bring the proportional balance of your portfolio holdings (the percentage of each asset type you wish to hold) back to their desired relationship.

Risk: A very controversial term that everyone seems to understand in general but experts can't agree on in specifics. Ultimately, it has to do with the likelihood of losing your invested capital.

Roth: Senator William Roth Jr. from Delaware was instrumental in crafting and helping to get passed the Taxpayer Relief Act of 1997 in which 401(k) plans and IRAs were offered in a modified form. In this new option, after-tax money could be deposited into these accounts and could then grow entirely tax-free, with no taxes imposed at any future point. Also, unlike their counterparts, Roth accounts do not have required minimum distributions.

Rule of 72: A shorthand method of determining the length of time in which your investment will double based upon dividing the integer of the interest rate into the number 72. For instance, if you were earning 7% interest (compounded annually), by dividing 7 into 72 you get 10.28, which is the number of years it would take for your investment to double.

Sectors (Market Sectors): A term used to describe a specific portion of the economy. This is a broader term than industry, as there are several industries within a sector. For example, in the medical sector are the pharmaceutical, biotechnology, health care, and medical equipment industries.

Security: Any form of tradable financial asset.

Seed Capital: The initial money used to start a business.

Short: Being involved in an investment in which you profit if the price of your holding goes down. (see **Long**)

Speculation: Putting one's money into any investment vehicle without the requisite amount of prior research, introspection, intelligence, forethought, experience, and control. For instance, simply buying a stock on a "hot tip" or because one feels it will "go up" is pure speculation. There are very few ways to separate oneself from one's money faster.

Spot Price: The live market valuation of a precious metal. This is usually below the price you are able to buy such an item for, however, as there are commissions to be added.

Spread: The difference in the rate of return of *two different investments*, or the difference in the rate of return of the same investment offered in *two different markets*, or the difference between the *bid* and the *ask* price of a security.

Stagflation: The economic condition in which both a high inflation rate and high unemployment occur at the same time. Certain economic theories (the Phillips curve) suggest this can't happen, yet it does.

Stagnation: A flat economy with sideways markets (no real increase or decrease in security values).

Stocks: A sliver of ownership in a corporation. Stocks are sold in individual shares, conferring on the shareholder the right to receive dividends, capital appreciation (or depreciation) in the price of each share, or both.

Style Investing: The building of a diversified portfolio of stocks by mixing growth, value, and blend stocks in one perspective and small, mid, and large cap stocks in another.

Tax-Advantaged Account: Any type of vehicle for saving money in which the government has conferred some type of tax advantage. These can include IRAs, 401(k)s (and their equivalents for tax-exempt and government organizations), 529 savings accounts, and health savings accounts (HSAs).

Taxes: We don't really need to define this, we know, but we can't pass up a chance to tell you how much you will hate them as you go beyond financial fitness. However, always pay your sovereign governments their due, correctly, and on time. Don't mess around here or try to be cute with something so grave.

Term Life Insurance: A life insurance product that has low premiums but offers only a benefit payable upon death. Also, as the name suggests, this type of life insurance is only valid for a certain time, usually twenty-five years. (see **Permanent Life Insurance**)

Treasury Bill (T-Bills): A short-term debt obligation backed by the U.S. government with a maturity of less than one year. They trade at a discount and do not pay interest. The return on Treasury Bills is determined by the difference between the price the investor paid and the price at which the investor sells or redeems it.

Treasury Bond: A marketable U.S. government debt security with a fixed interest rate and a maturity of over 10 years. Interest on Treasury Bonds is paid every six months.

Treasury Inflation Protected Security (T.I.P.S.): A marketable U.S. government debt security that is indexed to inflation in order to protect investors from the negative effects of inflation.

Treasury Note: A marketable U.S. government debt security with a fixed interest rate and a maturity between one and 10 years. Interest on Treasury Notes is paid every six months.

Umbrella Liability Insurance Policy: Extra liability coverage that protects the bearer beyond the normal limits of his/her home, car, boat insurance. It provides an additional level of protection to those who may be in danger of being sued for damage to someone else's property or injury.

Value Stock: A stock from a company paying solid dividends, with solid earnings, but with little expectation of gaining significant market share in the future. These are usually more mature companies in stable sectors. These stocks are often said to be "cheap" or of "good value." (see **Growth Stock**)

Volatility: The extent to which a particular asset fluctuates in price relative to the greater market.

Will and Testament: The legal document by which you identify the individuals and/or charities that are to receive your possessions upon your death.

YOU, Inc.: A term used to convey the need for a person to view himself or herself as a business that needs to be built into a stronger and more profitable entity over time.

YOU, Inc. Investment Hierarchy: A device that demonstrates a priority relationship between various possible assets in which one can invest. The bottom levels are the largest and therefore the most important. The higher levels represent increased sophistication, lesser importance, and usually higher risk.

ACKNOWLEDGEMENTS

Books are not written so much as they are built. And in the construction of this one, many people rolled up their sleeves and helped make it a reality. First of all we wish to thank the fanatically dedicated staff at Obstaclés Press, Inc., especially Michelle Turner and Bill Rousseau, who chase details and hold us to deadlines as only they can. Randy Robson also deserves special thanks for great work with the arrangement of the workbook. Norm Williams, after sixteen years of working with us, only gets better at reading our minds and creating graphical magic. We also wish to thank Ryan Renz, Andy Garcia, Jordan Woodward, Steve Kendall, Chris Janes, Jenn Headley, Gabby Theriot, Nathalie Miller, and the rest of the media department who produced the audio and video training aids (in multiple languages) that bring the material in this book to life. Rob Hallstrand deserves a merit badge for all his many hours of dedication and impressive ability to make it look easy. Thanks also to Bill Sankbeil for always having our back. As for our partners Claude and Lana Hamilton, Bill and Keisha Lewis, Dan and Lisa Hawkins, George and Jill Guzzardo, Rob and Kenyon Robson, and Thierry and Mary-Maude Laplanche, we consider it one of life's highest privileges to be able to work with you on a regular basis. You are consummate professionals and rascals at the same time! And finally, to our wives Terri Brady and Laurie Woodward, we don't know how you do it, but we sure are glad that you do. God truly blessed us when He put us together, and we praise Him for it!

FINANCIAL FITNESS PROGRAM

You've Worked Enough for Money,
Now It's Time to Get It Working for You!

FREE PERSONAL WEBSITE

SIGN UP AND TAKE ADVANTAGE OF THESE FREE FEATURES:

- Personal website
- Take your custom assessment test
- Build your own profile
- Share milestones and successes with partners and friends
- Post videos and photos
- Receive daily info "nuggets"

FINANCIAL FITNESS BASIC PROGRAM

The first program to teach all three aspects of personal finance: defense, offense, and playing field. Learn the simple, easy-to-apply principles that can help you shore up your resources, get out of debt, and build stability for a more secure future. It's all here, including a comprehensive book, companion workbook, and 8 audios that amplify the teachings from the books.

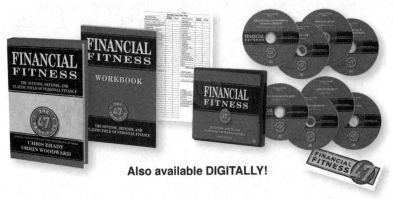

Also available DIGITALLY!

financialfitnessinfo.com

FINANCIAL FITNESS MASTER CLASS

Buy it once and use it forever! Designed to provide a continual follow-up to the principles learned in the Basic Program, this ongoing educational support offers over 6 hours of video and over 14 hours of audio instruction that walk you through the workbook, step by step. Perfect for individual or group study.
6 videos, 15 audios

FINANCIAL FITNESS TRACK AND SAVE

The Financial Fitness Program teaches you how to get out of debt, build additional streams of income, and properly take advantage of tax deductions. Now, with this subscription, we give you the tools to do so. The Tracker offers mobile expense tracking tools and budgeting software, while the Saver offers you thousands of coupons and discounts to help you save money every day.

THE WEALTH HABITS SERIES

The Wealth Habits series is designed to help you prosper through consistent, ongoing, simple, and enjoyable financial literacy education. You will learn timeless principles about how to better handle your money, and timely commentary on the current economic forces affecting the "playing field" upon which we all must participate. Small doses of information applied consistently over time can produce enormous results through the formation of new and profitable habits. This is what the Wealth Habits series is all about.

The Wealth Habits series will put you in a unique position. You will know something that only a few people in the world know. You will know the principles of financial fitness. You have the power to not only develop financial fitness but also to positively impact the lives of those around you. And the time to act is NOW.

LEARN TO NOT ONLY *SURVIVE*, BUT *THRIVE* DURING TOUGH ECONOMIC TIMES!

BEYOND FINANCIAL FITNESS PROGRAM

The original Financial Fitness program taught all three aspects of personal finance:defense, offense, and playing field. Now, the long anticipated Beyond Financial Fitness builds on that platform by teaching how to maximize the potential of your various streams of income by properly accumulating an ever-growing portfolio of cash-flow-producing assets.

Drawn from many of the greatest minds in the history of personal finance, the Beyond Financial Fitness program teaches you to gain mastery over your money once and for all and includes a comprehensive book, audio version of the book, a companion workbook, 4 audios, and 2 DVDs. Bookmark and decal also included. *You've worked enough for money, now it's time to get it working for you!*

Also available DIGITALLY!

financialfitnessinfo.com